Ninja Speedi Cookbook for Beginners:

365 Days of Quick, Flavor-Packed Recipes | Unleashing the Full Potential of Your Multi-Cooker for Effortless Meals Every Day

By:
Kieran Ellis

Table of Contents

Introduction

In the culinary world, where flavors fuse as well as ingredients dance harmoniously, there exists a remarkable realm of artistry as well as innovation. It's a place where creativity is your sous chef, as well as imagination is your secret ingredient. It's a realm where speed meets skill, where you can whip up a delectable masterpiece in the blink of an eye. Welcome to the exhilarating world of the Ninja Speedi Cookbook.

Imagine this: You walk into your kitchen after a long, exhausting day at work. The clock is ticking, as well as your stomach growls with impatience. The thought of slaving over a hot stove for hours is the last thing you want. What if we told you that you could prepare a gourmet meal in mere Min? Sounds like a culinary dream, doesn't it?

Enter the Ninja Speedi Cookbook—a revolutionary guide that will transform your kitchen into a hub of excitement, efficiency, as well as mouthwatering flavors. Whether you're a novice cook looking to impress your friends, a busy professional craving delicious home-cooked meals, or a seasoned chef seeking new as well as exciting culinary adventures, this cookbook is your golden ticket to a world of speedy gastronomic delights.

Picture a ninja poised for action, ready to strike with precision as well as speed. That's the essence of Ninja Speedi Cooking. It's all about mastering the art of swift as well as skillful cooking, combining the principles of ninja agility with culinary finesse. In this cookbook, you'll embark on a culinary journey that will elevate your cooking game to ninja status.

But what sets the Ninja Speedi Cookbook apart from the myriad of cookbooks lining the shelves? To answer that question, we need to delve deeper into its captivating essence.

Think about the last time you treated yourself to a restaurant-quality meal. The flavors were exquisite, the presentation flawless, but the bill? Not so much. With the Ninja Speedi Cookbook, you can recreate those unforgettable dining experiences in the comfort of your own home, without the hefty price tag.

We believe that the most delightful meals don't require endless hours of preparation. Instead, they demas well as a deep understas well asing of ingredients, an appreciation for culinary techniques, as well as the swift execution of a ninja. Our cookbook is your gateway to crafting restaurant-worthy dishes in Min. From sizzling stir-fries to succulent steaks, mouthwatering pastas to heavenly desserts, every recipe has been carefully crafted to deliver a symphony of flavors that will leave your taste buds singing.

In today's fast-paced world, time is a precious commodity. We understas well as that you have a hundred things on your to-do list, as well as spending hours in the kitchen isn't always feasible. That's where the Ninja Speedi Cookbook comes to the rescue. Our recipes are designed to streamline your cooking process, allowing you to prepare meals efficiently without sacrificing taste or quality.

But it's not just about speed; it's also about innovation. The Ninja Speedi Cookbook is your culinary laboratory, where you'll experiment with cutting-edge kitchen gadgets as well as techniques that will revolutionize your cooking. From air frying as well as pressure cooking to sous-vide as well as quick pickling, you'll learn how to harness the power of modern kitchen tools to your advantage.

Whether you're a culinary newbie or a seasoned pro, the Ninja Speedi Cookbook has something to offer. For beginners, our cookbook provides a gentle introduction to the world of cooking, guiding you through fundamental techniques as well as building your confidence one recipe at a time. For experienced cooks, it's an opportunity to push your culinary boundaries, explore new flavor profiles, as well as master the art of efficient cooking.

We firmly believe that anyone can become a ninja in the kitchen, armed with the right knowledge as well as a dash of courage. Our cookbook is your sensei, imparting wisdom as well as guidance to help you navigate the world of culinary creativity with ease as well as finesse.

Beyond the practicality as well as speed, cooking is an adventure—a journey that takes you to far-off las well ass, introduces you to diverse cultures, as well as tantalizes your taste buds with exotic flavors. The Ninja Speedi Cookbook is your passport to this exciting culinary expedition.

From the bustling streets of Bangkok to the romantic alleys of Paris, from the fiery kitchens of Mexico to the serene tea houses of Japan, our cookbook spans the globe, bringing you a treasure trove of recipes inspired by cuisines from every corner of the world. Each dish is a window into a different culture, a culinary snapshot that allows you to explore, savor, as well as appreciate the rich tapestry of global flavors.

Throughout the Ninja Speedi Cookbook, you'll find more than just recipes. You'll discover the ninja wisdom that guides the culinary world's most agile as well as skilled practitioners. From time-saving tips as well as kitchen hacks to ingredient substitutions as well as flavor pairings, this cookbook is a comprehensive resource that empowers you to cook with confidence as well as creativity.

Moreover, we understas well as that dietary preferences as well as restrictions vary, which is why our cookbook offers a wide range of recipes to suit different needs. Whether you're a carnivore, vegetarian, vegan, or gluten-free enthusiast, you'll find a plethora of options to cater to your specific tastes as well as dietary requirements.

The Ninja Speedi Cookbook is not just a cookbook; it's a movement—a culinary revolution that invites you to break free from the shackles of time-consuming cooking as well as embrace the art of ninja-inspired cuisine. It's a celebration of the joy that comes from creating delicious meals quickly as well as effortlessly.

So, are you ready to embark on this exhilarating culinary journey? Are you prepared to wield your kitchen tools with the skill of a ninja as well as whip up gourmet dishes in the blink of an eye? The Ninja Speedi Cookbook awaits, ready to guide you on a path of culinary mastery, efficiency, as well as, above all, deliciousness. It's time to unleash your inner ninja chef as well as experience the magic of speedi cooking like never before. Get ready to savor the adventure, one speedy bite at a time.

Chapter 1:
The history of the Ninja Speedi

The history of the Ninja Speedi, a revolutionary approach to fast as well as efficient cooking, is a tale of culinary innovation as well as a response to the ever-increasing demas well ass of our fast-paced modern lives. While there isn't a specific historical timeline for the concept of Ninja Speedi cooking, we can trace its origins as well as development through several key milestones in the world of culinary arts as well as technology.

1. Emergence of Fast Food Culture:

- The concept of fast food can be considered an early precursor to Ninja Speedi cooking. In the mid-20th century, fast-food restaurants like McDonald's as well as KFC introduced the idea of quickly prepared, ready-to-eat meals, catering to people's desire for convenient as well as speedy dining options.

2. Introduction of Microwave Ovens:

- In the 1950s, the microwave oven was invented, marking a significant milestone in kitchen technology. It allowed for rapid heating as well as cooking of various dishes, reducing the time required for meal preparation.

3. Rise of Convenience Foods:

- The latter half of the 20th century saw the proliferation of convenience foods, such as frozen dinners, instant noodles, as well as pre-packaged sauces. These products were designed to simplify cooking as well as reduce the time needed to prepare meals.

4. Fusion Cuisine as well as Cross-Cultural Influences:

- As globalization continued to bring diverse culinary traditions closer together, fusion cuisine emerged. Chefs began combining flavors as well as techniques from different cultures, often resulting in innovative as well as speedy dishes that drew from various culinary traditions.

5. The Advent of Kitchen Gadgets:

- Advances in kitchen gadgets as well as appliances, such as food processors, pressure cookers, as well as sous-vide machines, played a pivotal role in speeding up the cooking process. These tools allowed for efficient food preparation as well as precise cooking techniques, even for complex dishes.

6. The Internet as well as Sharing of Recipes:

- With the rise of the internet as well as social media, home cooks gained access to an abundance of recipes, cooking tips, as well as tutorials. This democratization of culinary knowledge allowed individuals to experiment with new recipes as well as cooking methods, often prioritizing speed as well as convenience.

7. The Ninja Speedi Cookbook:

- While there isn't a single "Eureka!" moment for Ninja Speedi cooking, the emergence of the Ninja Speedi Cookbook as a concept as well as guide marked a significant milestone. This cookbook brought together the principles of speed, efficiency, as well as culinary finesse, offering a wide range of recipes as well as techniques designed to help home cooks prepare gourmet meals in a fraction of the time it would traditionally take.

8. Evolution of Speedi Cooking Techniques:

- As Ninja Speedi cooking gained popularity, it evolved to incorporate various time-saving techniques, such as air frying, pressure cooking, as well as quick pickling. These methods allowed for the rapid preparation of dishes without compromising on taste or quality.

9. Popularization of Healthy as well as Quick Cooking:

- The health-conscious trend of preparing nutritious meals quickly also contributed to the growth of Ninja Speedi cooking. This movement emphasized fresh ingredients, smart cooking techniques, as well as balanced nutrition, aligning with the ethos of Ninja Speedi cooking.

10. Ongoing Culinary Innovation: - Ninja Speedi cooking continues to evolve with ongoing culinary innovation, advancements in kitchen technology, as well as the dynamic nature of food culture. It remains a reflection of our ever-changing lifestyles, where efficiency as well as flavor coexist in perfect harmony.

Chapter 2:
Ninja Speedi techniques

Ninja Speedi techniques are a set of culinary skills as well as strategies designed to streamline cooking processes, reduce preparation time, as well as deliver delicious results quickly. These techniques are inspired by the agility as well as precision of ninjas as well as are perfect for anyone looking to master the art of fast as well as efficient cooking. Here are some key Ninja Speedi techniques:

1. Mise en Place (Everything in Its Place):

- Before you start cooking, gather as well as prepare all your ingredients. Chop vegetables, measure spices, as well as have everything ready to go. This technique ensures you won't waste time searching for ingredients while cooking.

2. Knife Skills:

- Sharpen your knife skills to reduce prep time. Learn to chop, dice, as well as slice quickly as well as safely. A sharp knife makes all the difference.

3. One-Pot as well as One-Pan Meals:

- Opt for recipes that allow you to cook everything in a single pot or pan. This minimizes cleanup as well as speeds up the cooking process.

4. Batch Cooking:

- Cook in huge batches as well as store leftovers for future meals. This is especially useful for busy weekdays when you don't have time to cook from scratch.

5. Pre-Marinating Proteins:

- Marinate proteins (like chicken or tofu) in advance to infuse them with flavor. This cuts down on cooking time as well as ensures your dish is packed with taste.

6. High-Heat Cooking:

- Use high-heat cooking methods like stir-frying, searing, or sautéing to cook food quickly while retaining its natural flavors as well as textures.

7. Sheet Pan as well as Tray Baking:

- Arrange ingredients on a sheet pan or tray, season them, as well as roast in the oven. This method allows for has well ass-free cooking while everything cooks together.

8. Pressure Cooking:

- Invest in a pressure cooker, which can significantly reduce cooking time for dishes that typically take a long time, such as stews or braised meats.

9. Air Frying:

- An air fryer circulates hot air to cook food quickly as well as with less oil. It's perfect for achieving crispy textures in a fraction of the time.

10. Sous-Vide Cooking: - Sous-vide involves vacuum-sealing ingredients as well as cooking them in a precisely controlled water bath. While it requires longer cook times, it's has well ass-off as well as delivers restaurant-quality results with minimal effort.

11. Quick Pickling: - Add a burst of flavor to dishes with quick pickling. Submerge finely diced vegetables in a vinegar-based brine for a few Min to infuse them with tanginess as well as crunch.

12. Instant Pot Magic: - The Instant Pot is a versatile appliance that combines multiple cooking functions in one. It can pressure cook, slow cook, sauté, as well as more, significantly reducing cooking times.

13. Use Pre-Cooked Ingredients needed: - Incorporate pre-cooked or pre-packaged ingredients like pre-cooked rice, canned beans, or pre-marinated tofu to save time on meal preparation.

14. Kitchen Gadgets as well as Appliances: - Invest in time-saving kitchen gadgets like food processors, blender/food processor combos, as well as electric choppers to quickly prepare ingredients.

15. Simplicity in Seasoning: - Keep your seasoning straightforward as well as well-balanced. Focus on a few key flavors that complement each other rather than complex spice blends.

16. Freezing Ingredients needed: - Freeze ingredients like fruits, vegetables, as well as herbs when they're in season or on sale. This ensures you always have fresh ingredients on has well as.

17. Efficient Cleanup: - As you cook, clean as you go. Put away ingredients, wash dishes, as well as wipe down surfaces to maintain an organized as well as efficient workspace.

Chapter 3:
The Ninja Speedi advantages

The Ninja Speedi cooking approach offers numerous advantages for home cooks, making it a popular choice for those seeking efficient, delicious, as well as time-saving meal preparation. Here are some of the key advantages of the Ninja Speedi method:

1. **Time Efficiency:** Perhaps the most significant advantage of Ninja Speedi cooking is its ability to reduce cooking time significantly. This is particularly beneficial for busy individuals or families with limited time to spend in the kitchen. Ninja Speedi techniques as well as kitchen gadgets, like pressure cookers as well as air fryers, allow you to prepare meals in a fraction of the time it would traditionally take.

2. **Convenience:** Ninja Speedi cooking emphasizes convenience by streamlining the cooking process. It encourages the use of one-pot as well as one-pan meals, batch cooking, as well as pre-prepared ingredients, minimizing the number of dishes to wash as well as simplifying meal planning.

3. **Versatility:** Ninja Speedi cooking is incredibly versatile. Whether you're interested in preparing breakfast, lunch, dinner, or snacks, the techniques as well as recipes can be adapted to a wide range of culinary needs as well as preferences.

4. **Consistent Results:** With precision cooking methods like sous-vide, pressure cooking, as well as air frying, Ninja Speedi cooking offers consistent as well as

reliable results. Your dishes are less likely to be overcooked or undercooked, ensuring that your food is perfectly cooked every time.

5. **Nutrient Retention:** Speedy cooking methods like pressure cooking as well as steaming help retain more of the nutrients in your ingredients compared to traditional methods that might involve longer cooking times or excessive heat.
6. **Flavorful Meals:** Ninja Speedi cooking doesn't sacrifice flavor for speed. In fact, it often enhances flavor by concentrating as well as locking in the natural tastes of ingredients. Quick pickling as well as marinating techniques also infuse dishes with delicious flavors.
7. **Energy Efficiency:** Many Ninja Speedi techniques, such as air frying as well as pressure cooking, are energy-efficient. They use less electricity or gas compared to extended stovetop or oven cooking, which can result in energy savings as well as lower utility bills.
8. **Healthier Choices:** The emphasis on fresh ingredients as well as quick cooking methods encourages healthier eating. Ninja Speedi cooking allows you to avoid relying on pre-packaged, processed foods as well as instead create nutritious meals at home.
9. **Reduced Food Waste:** Batch cooking as well as using leftovers from one meal in the next can help reduce food waste, as you're more likely to use all the ingredients you buy.
10. **Cost Savings:** By cooking at home more efficiently as well as reducing reliance on takeout or dining out, you can save money in the long run. Additionally, buying ingredients in bulk as well as using leftovers wisely can further reduce food expenses.
11. **Variety as well as Creativity:** Ninja Speedi cooking doesn't limit your culinary creativity. In fact, it encourages experimentation with flavors, ingredients, as well as techniques, allowing you to explore a wide range of dishes as well as cuisines quickly.
12. **Accessible to All Skill Levels:** Ninja Speedi techniques can be tailored to suit all skill levels, from beginners to experienced cooks. The approach accommodates those with limited cooking experience while also providing opportunities for seasoned chefs to expas well as their repertoire.

Chapter 4:
The Ninja Speedi Maintenance

Maintaining your Ninja Speedi kitchen setup is crucial to ensure that your cooking remains efficient, safe, as well as enjoyable. Proper maintenance not only extends the lifespan of your kitchen appliances as well as tools but also helps you continue to prepare delicious meals quickly. Here are some maintenance tips to consider:

1. Regular Cleaning:

- Clean your kitchen appliances as well as tools after each use. This includes cleaning your air fryer, pressure cooker, blender, food processor, as well as any other gadgets you use in your Ninja Speedi cooking. Follow the manufacturer's instructions for cleaning to prevent any buildup of food residue, grease, or grime.

2. Deep Cleaning:

- Periodically, perform a deep cleaning of your kitchen appliances as well as gadgets. This may involve disassembling parts that can be removed (if safe to do so) as well as cleaning them thoroughly. For example, some pressure cookers have removable sealing rings that need regular cleaning.

3. Check for Wear as well as Tear:

- Routinely inspect your kitchen tools as well as appliances for signs of wear as well as tear. Look for cracks, frayed cords, or any other damage that might compromise safety or performance. Replace damaged parts promptly.

4. Sharpen Blades:

- Keep the blades of your knives as well as food processors sharp. Dull blades can slow down your cooking as well as increase the risk of accidents. Regularly sharpen your knives as well as follow the manufacturer's recommendations for maintaining the sharpness of other blades.

5. Lubricate Moving Parts:

- If your kitchen gadgets have moving parts, such as a food processor's blade assembly, lubricate them according to the manufacturer's instructions. This helps ensure smooth operation as well as prolongs the life of the appliance.

6. Store Properly:

- Store your kitchen tools as well as appliances in a clean, dry, as well as safe place. Avoid exposing them to extreme temperatures or humidity, which can affect their performance as well as longevity.

7. Replace Seals as well as Gaskets:

- For appliances like pressure cookers or blenders that have seals or gaskets, regularly check for signs of wear or damage. Replace these components as needed to maintain the appliance's functionality as well as safety.

8. Follow Manufacturer's Guidelines:

- Always adhere to the manufacturer's recommendations for maintenance as well as care. These guidelines can be found in the user manuals that come with your kitchen appliances as well as tools.

9. Descale as Needed:

- If you have a kitchen gadget that uses water, such as a coffee maker or electric kettle, follow the manufacturer's instructions for descaling to prevent mineral buildup.

10. Store Ingredients Properly: - Pay attention to the storage of ingredients. Keep dry goods in airtight containers to maintain freshness, as well as store perishables in the refrigerator or freezer as needed to prevent spoilage.

11. Keep an Organized Kitchen: - Maintain an organized kitchen to streamline your cooking process. Knowing where everything is as well as having easy access to your tools as well as ingredients can save you time as well as reduce stress while cooking.

12. Learn as well as Adapt: - Continuously educate yourself about your kitchen gadgets as well as appliances. Keep up to date with any recalls or safety recommendations from the manufacturer.

13. Safety First: - Prioritize safety in your kitchen. Always follow safety guidelines as well as use caution when has well asling hot appliances or sharp tools.

Chapter 5:
Ninja speedi cooker Breakfast Recipes

- Preparation Period: 5 Min
- Cooking Period: 5 Min
- Serves: 2

Ingredients needed:

- 4 huge eggs
- 1/4 C. full of diced spinach
- 2 tbsps.full of crumbled feta cheese
- Pepper as well as sea salt, as desired.

Preparation process

1. The eggs should be cracked into a bowl as well as thoroughly mixed.
2. Season the eggs with sea salt as well as pepper before adding the feta cheese as well as diced spinach.
3. Set the sauté setting on your Ninja Speedi Rapid Cooker to preheat.

4. When the eggs are cooked to the appropriate doneness, pour the egg mixture into the cooker as well as stir gently.
5. Serve right away.

Serving Total

- Kcal:180
- Carbs: 1g
- Fat: 14g
- Protein: 13g

2. Speedy Banana Oatmeal

- Preparation Period: 2 Min
- Cooking Period: 3 Min
- Serves: 1

Ingredients needed:

- 1/2 C. full of rolled oats
- 1 ripe banana, mashed
- 1/2 C. full of almond milk
- 1 tbsp.full of honey
- 1/2 tsp. full of cinnamon
- Diced bananas as well as diced nuts for topping (optional)

Preparation process

1. Rolling oats, banana puree, almond milk, honey, as well as cinnamon are all combined in a bowl.
2. Set the porridge setting on your Ninja Speedi Rapid Cooker to preheat.
3. When the oatmeal mixture has reached the proper thickness, pour it into the cooker as well as cook, stirring occasionally.
4. Before serving, top with diced nuts as well as banana slices, if preferred.

Serving Total

- Kcal:350

- Carbs: 70g
- Fat: 6g
- Protein: 7g

3. Veggie Omelette

- Preparation Period: 7 Min
- Cooking Period: 5 Min
- Serves: 2

Ingredients needed:

- 4 huge eggs
- 1/4 C. full of diced bell peppers
- 1/4 C. full of diced onions
- 1/4 C. full of diced tomatoes
- 1/4 C. full of diced cheddar cheese
- Pepper as well as sea salt, as desired.

Preparation process

1. In a bowl, beat the eggs thoroughly. Add some pepper as well as sea salt.
2. Set the sauté setting on your Ninja Speedi Rapid Cooker to preheat.
3. After adding the diced vegetables, pour the beaten eggs into the cooker.
4. Cheese should be sprinkled on top after cooking the eggs with intermittent tossing until they are almost set.
5. Cook the omelette until the cheese is melted after folding it in half.
6. Serve warm.

Serving Total

- Kcal:210
- Carbs: 6g
- Fat: 15g
- Protein: 13g

- Preparation Period: 10 Min
- Cooking Period: 5 Min
- Serves: 2

Ingredients needed:

- 4 huge eggs
- 1/4 C. full of diced ham
- 1/4 C. full of diced bell peppers
- 1/4 C. full of diced onions
- 1/4 C. full of diced cheddar cheese
- 2 huge flour tortillas
- pepper as well as sea salt, as desired.

Preparation process

1. Whisk the eggs in a bowl as well as season with sea salt as well as pepper.
2. Preheat your Ninja Speedi Rapid Cooker on the sauté function.
3. Add diced ham, bell peppers, as well as onions to the cooker. Cook until they soften.
4. Pour the beaten eggs into the cooker as well as stir until they're cooked to your liking.
5. Warm the tortillas in the cooker.
6. Spoon the egg mixture onto the tortillas, sprinkle with cheese, as well as fold into burritos.
7. Serve immediately.

Serving Total

- Kcal:390
- Carbs: 23g
- Fat: 25g
- Protein: 20g

- Preparation Period: 5 Min
- Cooking Period: 5 Min
- Serves: 2

Ingredients needed:

- 4 slices of bread
- 2 huge eggs
- 1/4 C. full of milk
- 1/2 tsp. full of vanilla extract
- 1/2 tsp. full of cinnamon
- Butter for frying (optional)
- Maple syrup as well as fresh berries for topping

Preparation process

1. Combine the eggs, milk, vanilla, as well as cinnamon in a bowl.
2. Set the griddle setting on your Ninja Speedi Rapid Cooker to preheat.
3. Coat both sides of each slice of bread by dipping it into the egg mixture.
4. The bread slices should be cooked in the cooker until both sides are golden brown.
5. Serve with some fresh berries, maple syrup, as well as butter.

Serving Total

- Kcal:280
- Carbs: 38g
- Fat: 9g
- Protein: 10g

- Preparation Period: 5 Min
- Cooking Period: 3 Min
- Serves: 1

Ingredients needed:

- 1 huge whole wheat tortilla
- 2 tbsps.full of peanut butter
- 1 banana, diced
- Honey for drizzling (optional)

Preparation process

1. On the whole wheat tortilla, evenly distribute the peanut butter.
2. Place banana slices in the center of the tortilla.
3. If desired, drizzle honey on top of the bananas.
4. The tortilla is rolled up as well as divided in half.
5. Serve right away.

Serving Total

- Kcal:380
- Carbs: 56g
- Fat: 14g
- Protein: 10g

7.   Speedy Breakfast Quesadilla

- Preparation Period: 5 Min
- Cooking Period: 5 Min
- Serves: 2

Ingredients needed:

- 4 huge eggs
- 2 huge whole wheat tortillas
- 1/2 C. full of diced cheddar cheese
- 1/4 C. full of diced ham
- Pepper as well as sea salt, as desired.

Preparation process

1. Add sea salt as well as pepper to a bowl with the whisked eggs.

2. Set the sauté setting on your Ninja Speedi Rapid Cooker to preheat.
3. In the cooker, add the beaten eggs, as well as scramble them until they are thoroughly cooked.
4. One tortilla should be placed in the cooker along with half of the scrambled eggs, ham, as well as diced cheese.
5. Then, gently press the second tortilla on top.
6. Cook the tortillas as well as cheese until they are both crispy.
7. Cut into wedges as well as serve.

Serving Total

- Kcal:380
- Carbs: 22g
- Fat: 24g
- Protein: 21g

8. Speedi Greek Yogurt Parfait

- Preparation Period: 3 Min
- Cooking Period: 0 Min
- Serves: 1

Ingredients needed:

- 1 C. full of Greek yogurt
- 1/2 C. full of mixed berries (strawberries, blueberries, raspberries)
- 2 tbsps.full of honey
- 2 tbsps.full of granola

Preparation process

1. Greek yogurt, granola, as well as mixed berries should be arranged in a glass or bowl.
2. Honey should be drizzled on top.
3. Serve right away.

Serving Total

- Kcal:340
- Carbs: 49g
- Fat: 7g
- Protein: 21g

9. Speedy Avocado Toast

- Preparation Period: 5 Min
- Cooking Period: 3 Min
- Serves: 2

Ingredients needed:

- 2 slices whole wheat bread
- 1 ripe avocado, mashed
- Cherry tomatoes, diced
- Flakes of red pepper(optional)
- Pepper as well as sea salt, as desired.

Preparation process

1. With the help of your Ninja Speedi Rapid Cooker, toast the slices of whole wheat bread.
2. On the toasted bread slices, equally distribute the mashed avocado.
3. Add diced cherry tomatoes on top.
4. Season with sea salt as well as pepper, as well as top with red pepper flakes (if preferred).
5. Serve right away.

Serving Total

- Kcal:210
- Carbs: 24g
- Fat: 11g
- Protein: 5g

- Preparation Period: 5 Min
- Cooking Period: 0 Min
- Serves: 1

Ingredients needed:

- 1 ripe banana
- 1/2 C. full of frozen berries (strawberries, blueberries, or mixed berries)
- 1/2 C. full of Greek yogurt
- 1/2 C. full of almond milk
- 1 tbsp.full of honey (optional)
- 1/2 tsp. full of vanilla extract (optional)
- Ice cubes (optional)

Preparation process

1. Blend together all the ingredients.
2. Blend till creamy as well as smooth.
3. If you like a cooler smoothie, add ice cubes.
4. Pour into a glass as well as enjoy right away..

Serving Total

- Kcal:290
- Carbs: 54g
- Fat: 3g
- Protein: 14g

11. Speedy Veggie Breakfast Burrito Bowl

- Preparation Period: 10 Min
- Cooking Period: 5 Min
- Serves: 2

Ingredients needed:

- 4 huge eggs
- 1/2 C. full of diced bell peppers
- 1/4 C. full of diced onions
- 1/4 C. full of diced tomatoes
- 1/4 C. full of black beans, drained as well as rinsed
- 1/4 C. full of diced cheddar cheese
- Pepper as well as sea salt, as desired.
- Salsa as well as avocado slices for topping (optional)

Preparation process

1. The eggs should be whisked in a bowl with sea salt as well as pepper.
2. Set the sauté setting on your Ninja Speedi Rapid Cooker to preheat.
3. To the cooker, add diced bell peppers, onions, as well as tomatoes. Until they soften, cook.
4. When the eggs are cooked to your preference, pour the beaten eggs into the cooker as well as stir.
5. Divide the egg mixture into two bowls, then assemble the burrito bowls.
6. Add black beans, cheese, as well as any additional preferred garnishes, such as salsa as well as avocado slices.
7. Serve warm.

Serving Total

- Kcal:280
- Carbs: 15g
- Fat: 18g
- Protein: 17g

12. Speedi Spinach and Mushroom Breakfast Quesadilla

- Preparation Period: 7 Min
- Cooking Period: 5 Min
- Serves: 2

Ingredients needed:

- 4 huge eggs
- 2 huge whole wheat tortillas
- 1 C. full of fresh spinach leaves
- 1/2 C. full of diced mushrooms
- 1/4 C. full of diced mozzarella cheese
- Pepper as well as sea salt, as desired.

Preparation process

1. Add sea salt as well as pepper to a bowl with the whisked eggs.
2. Set the sauté setting on your Ninja Speedi Rapid Cooker to preheat.
3. Cook the diced mushrooms in the cooker until they begin to turn brown.
4. When the eggs are thoroughly cooked as well as scrambled, pour the beaten eggs into the cooker as well as mix.
5. Place one tortilla in the cooker as well as top with mozzarella cheese, fresh spinach, as well as half of the egg mixture.
6. Then, gently press the second tortilla on top.
7. Cook the tortillas as well as cheese until they are both crispy.
8. Serve after cutting into wedges.

Serving Total

- Kcal:280
- Carbs: 24g
- Fat: 15g
- Protein: 17g

13. Speedy Breakfast Wrap with Smoked Salmon

- Preparation Period: 5 Min
- Cooking Period: 5 Min
- Serves: 1

Ingredients needed:

- 1 huge whole wheat tortilla

* 2 Oz. smoked salmon
* 2 tbsps.full of cream cheese
* 1/4 C. full of diced cucumber
* 1/4 C. full of baby spinach leaves
* Lemon zest for garnish (optional)

Preparation process

1. On the whole wheat tortilla, evenly distribute cream cheese.
2. Place slices of smoked salmon on top.
3. include tiny spinach leaves as well as diced cucumber.
4. The tortilla is rolled up as well as divided in half.
5. If desired, add lemon zest as a garnish.
6. Serve right away.

Serving Total

* Kcal:290
* Carbs: 24g
* Fat: 14g
* Protein: 19g

14. Speedi Blueberry Pancakes

* Preparation Period: 10 Min
* Cooking Period: 5 Min
* Serves: 2

Ingredients needed:

* 1 C. full of pancake mix
* 1/2 C. full of water
* 1/2 C. full of fresh blueberries
* Butter for frying (optional)
* Maple syrup for topping

Preparation process

1. Pancake mix as well as water should be thoroughly combined in a bowl.
2. Set the griddle setting on your Ninja Speedi Rapid Cooker to preheat.
3. The griddle should be butter-greased (if desired).
4. Small pancake rounds should be poured onto the griddle along with a few blueberries.
5. Cook until surface bubbles appear, then flip as well as continue to cook until golden brown.
6. Add maple syrup to the dish.

Serving Total

- Kcal:260
- Carbs: 59g
- Fat: 1g
- Protein: 4g

15. Speedy Breakfast Tacos

- Preparation Period: 10 Min
- Cooking Period: 5 Min
- Serves: 2

Ingredients needed:

- 4 huge eggs
- 4 small corn tortillas
- 1/2 C. full of cooked as well as crumbled sausage
- 1/4 C. full of diced tomatoes
- 1/4 C. full of diced onions
- 1/4 C. full of diced cheddar cheese
- Pepper as well as sea salt, as desired.
- Salsa as well as diced cilantro for topping (optional)

Preparation process

1. Add sea salt as well as pepper to a bowl with the whisked eggs.

2. Set the sauté setting on your Ninja Speedi Rapid Cooker to preheat.
3. To the cooker, add diced onions as well as tomatoes. Until they soften, cook.
4. When the eggs are thoroughly cooked as well as scrambled, pour the beaten eggs into the cooker as well as mix.
5. Corn tortillas are warmed in the cooker.
6. By dividing the egg mixture among the tortillas, assemble the tacos.
7. Sausage crumbles, cheese cubes, salsa, as well as diced cilantro are optional additions.
8. Serve warm.

Serving Total

- Kcal:340
- Carbs: 18g
- Fat: 22g
- Protein: 18g

16. Speedy Chocolate Peanut Butter Smoothie Bowl

- Preparation Period: 5 Min
- Cooking Period: 0 Min
- Serves: 1

Ingredients needed:

- 1 ripe banana
- 2 tbsps.full of peanut butter
- 1 tbsp.full of cocoa powder
- 1/2 C. full of almond milk
- 1/2 C. full of Greek yogurt
- Toppings: diced banana, granola, as well as chocolate chips

Preparation process

1. Banana, peanut butter, chocolate powder, almond milk, as well as Greek yogurt are all combined in a blender.
2. Blend till creamy as well as smooth.

3. The smoothie should be poured into a bowl as well as topped with granola, diced banana, as well as a few chocolate chips.
4. Serve right away.

Serving Total

- Kcal:380
- Carbs: 49g
- Fat: 17g
- Protein: 16g

17. Speedi Breakfast BLT Wrap

- Preparation Period: 10 Min
- Cooking Period: 5 Min
- Serves: 2

Ingredients needed:

- 4 huge eggs
- 2 huge whole wheat tortillas
- 4 strips of cooked bacon
- 1/2 C. full of diced tomatoes
- 1/2 C. full of baby spinach leaves
- Pepper as well as sea salt, as desired.
- Mayonnaise or avocado spread (optional)

Preparation process

1. Add sea salt as well as pepper to a bowl with the whisked eggs.
2. Set the sauté setting on your Ninja Speedi Rapid Cooker to preheat.
3. In the cooker, add the beaten eggs, as well as scramble until fully cooked.
4. In the cooker, preheat the whole-wheat tortillas.
5. Each tortilla should have two fried bacon slices on it.
6. Add a few baby spinach leaves, sliced tomatoes, as well as scrambled eggs.
7. If desired, put some mayo or avocado on top.
8. The tortillas should be rolled as well as then sliced in half.
9. Serve warm.

Serving Total

- Kcal:340
- Carbs: 20g
- Fat: 20g
- Protein: 19g

18. Speedy Breakfast Pizza

- Preparation Period: 10 Min
- Cooking Period: 5 Min
- Serves: 2

Ingredients needed:

- 2 huge whole wheat tortillas
- 1/2 C. full of pizza sauce
- 1/2 C. full of diced mozzarella cheese
- 4 huge eggs
- 1/4 C. full of diced bell peppers
- 1/4 C. full of diced onions
- Pepper as well as sea salt, as desired.
- Fresh basil leaves for topping (optional)

Preparation process

1. Set the griddle setting on your Ninja Speedi Rapid Cooker to preheat.
2. Place tortillas made with whole wheat on the griddle.
3. Each tortilla should have a uniform layer of pizza sauce.
4. Add some mozzarella cheese in the form of dice.
5. The eggs should be whisked in a bowl with sea salt as well as pepper.
6. Over the tortillas, evenly distribute the beaten eggs.
7. Add onion as well as bell pepper dice.
8. When the eggs are done as well as the tortillas are crispy, cover the griddle as well as continue cooking.
9. If desired, garnish with fresh basil leaves.
10. Serve after cutting into wedges.

Serving Total

- Kcal:380
- Carbs: 26g
- Fat: 19g
- Protein: 23g

19. Speedy Huevos Rancheros

- Preparation Period: 10 Min
- Cooking Period: 5 Min
- Serves: 2

Ingredients needed:

- 4 huge eggs
- 2 huge corn tortillas
- 1 C. full of canned refried beans
- 1/2 C. full of salsa
- 1/4 C. full of diced cheddar cheese
- Fresh cilantro for topping (optional)

Preparation process

1. Set the sauté setting on your Ninja Speedi Rapid Cooker to preheat.
2. Corn tortillas are warmed in the cooker.
3. Each tortilla should have a uniform layer of refried beans.
4. The eggs should be beaten in a bowl before being added to the stove.
5. Cook the eggs through in a scramble.
6. Put beans on top of scrambled eggs.
7. Add salsa to the eggs as well as top with cheddar cheese slivers.
8. Adding fresh cilantro on top is optional.
9. Serve warm.

Serving Total

- Kcal:340
- Carbs: 28g

- Fat: 17g
- Protein: 19g

20. Speedy Chia Pudding Parfait

- Preparation Period: 5 Min
- Cooking Period: 0 Min (needs to refrigerate)
- Serves: 1

Ingredients needed:

- 2 tbsps.full of chia seeds
- 1/2 C. full of almond milk
- 1/2 C. full of Greek yogurt
- 1/2 C. full of mixed berries (strawberries, blueberries, raspberries)
- 1 tbsp.full of honey (optional)
- Diced almonds for topping (optional)

Preparation process

1. Almond milk as well as chia seeds should be combined in a bowl. Stir thoroughly.
2. The mixture must be chilled for at least two hours or overnight for it to thicken.
3. Greek yogurt, mixed berries, as well as chia pudding should be arranged in a glass or bowl.
4. Add honey to the top as well as, if preferred, almond dice.
5. Offer cold.

Serving Total

- Kcal:290
- Carbs: 37g
- Fat: 9g
- Protein: 15g

Chapter 6:
Ninja Speedi Cooker Lunch Recipes

21. Ninja Speedi Rapid Cooker Chicken Stir-Fry

- Preparation Period: 15 Min
- Cooking Period: 10 Min
- Serves: 4

Ingredients needed:

- 1 lb (450g) boneless chicken breast, finely diced
- 2 C. full of mixed vegetables (bell peppers, broccoli, snap peas)
- 2 cloves of garlic, crushed
- 2 tbsp low-sodium soy sauce
- 1 tbsp sesame oil
- 1 tbsp olive oil
- 1 tsp ginger, crushed
- Pepper as well as sea salt, as desired.
- 2 C. full of cooked rice

Preparation process

1. Sea salt as well as pepper are used to season the chicken slices.
2. Set the SEAR/SAUTÉ function of the Ninja Speedi Rapid Cooker to warm up. Sauté garlic as well as olive oil together for one Min.
3. Slices of chicken should be added as well as cooked until golden brown.
4. Stir-fry the ginger as well as mixed vegetables for 3–4 Min, or until they are soft.
5. Cook for a further 2 Min after adding the soy sauce as well as sesame oil.
6. Over cooked rice, serve the chicken stir-fry.

Serving Total:

- Kcal:350
- Carbs: 40g
- Fat: 8g
- Protein: 30g

22. Ninja Speedi Rapid Cooker Beef and Broccoli

- Preparation Period: 15 Min
- Cooking Period: 15 Min
- Serves: 4

Ingredients needed:

- 1 lb (450g) flank steak, finely diced
- 2 C. full of broccoli florets
- 1/2 C. full of low-sodium soy sauce
- 1/4 C. full of brown sugar
- 2 cloves of garlic, crushed
- 1 tsp full of ginger, crushed
- 1 tbsp full of cornstarch
- 2 tbsp full of vegetable oil
- Cooked white rice

Preparation process

1. Combine soy sauce, brown sugar, ginger, garlic, as well as cornstarch in a bowl. Place aside.
2. Set the SEAR/SAUTÉ function of the Ninja Speedi Rapid Cooker to warm up. Include vegetable oil.
3. Add the beef dice as well as heat for 2 to 3 Min on each side, or until browned. Remove as well as reserve the beef.
4. Cook the broccoli in the cooker for 3–4 Min, or until it is tender.
5. Add the sauce to the cooker once the beef is back in it.
6. The sauce needs to thicken, so stir as well as heat for an additional 2 Min.
7. Over cooked white rice, please.

Serving Total:

- Kcal:400
- Carbs: 30g
- Fat: 15g
- Protein: 30g

23. Speedy Pork Carnitas Tacos

- Preparation Period: 20 Min
- Cooking Period: 20 Min
- Serves: 6

Ingredients needed:

- 2 lb.s pork shoulder, cut into chunks
- 2 tbsps.full of vegetable oil
- 1 onion, diced
- 3 cloves of garlic, crushed
- 1 tsp. full of cumin
- 1 tsp. full of oregano
- 1 tsp. full of powdered chili
- 1/2 C. full of orange juice
- 1/4 C. full of lime juice
- Pepper as well as sea salt, as desired.

- Tortillas, salsa, as well as toppings for serving

Preparation process

1. Heat the vegetable oil as well as switch the Ninja Speedi Rapid Cooker to the "Sauté" setting.
2. Add the pork chunks, then brown them thoroughly. Take out as well as place aside.
3. Diced onion as well as garlic should be added to the same cooker. until softened, sauté.
4. Add the cumin, oregano, powdered chili, orange as well as lime juices, sea salt, as well as pepper to the cooker once the pork is added back.
5. Choose "Pressure Cook" as well as cook for 15 Min.
6. Slice the pork, then put it in tortillas with your preferred salsa as well as garnishes.

Serving Total:

- Kcal:380
- Carbs: 15g
- Fat: 22g
- Protein: 30g

24. Speedy Turkey and Vegetable Soup

- Preparation Period: 15 Min
- Cooking Period: 20 Min
- Serves: 6

Ingredients needed:

- 1 lb. crushed turkey
- 1 tbsp.full of olive oil
- 1 onion, diced
- 2 carrots, diced
- 2 celery stalks, diced
- 1 zucchini, diced
- 4 C. full of chicken broth
- 1 can diced tomatoes

- 1 C. full of frozen corn
- 1 tsp. full of Italian seasoning
- Pepper as well as sea salt, as desired.

Preparation process

1. Heat olive oil as well as switch the Ninja Speedi Rapid Cooker to the "Sauté" setting.
2. Crushed turkey should be added as well as cooked until browned. Take out as well as place aside.
3. Add diced onion, carrots, celery, as well as zucchini to the same cooker. Cook for 3–4 Min.
4. Add the chicken stock, diced tomatoes, frozen corn, Italian seasoning, sea salt, as well as pepper to the cooker along with the turkey once again.
5. Choose "Pressure Cook" as well as cook for 10 Min.
6. Hot turkey as well as vegetable soup should be served.

Serving Total:

- Kcal:220
- Carbs: 15g
- Fat: 10g
- Protein: 18g

25. Speedy Mutton Curry

- Preparation Period: 20 Min
- Cooking Period: 25 Min
- Serves: 4

Ingredients needed:

- 1 lb. boneless mutton pieces
- 2 tbsps.full of vegetable oil
- 1 onion, finely diced
- 2 cloves of garlic, crushed
- 1-inch piece of ginger, crushed
- 2 tomatoes, diced

- 1 tsp. full of turmeric powder
- 1 tsp. full of coriander powder
- 1 tsp. full of cumin powder
- 1 tsp. full of garam masala
- Sea salt to taste
- Diced cilantro for garnish
- Cooked rice or naan for serving

Preparation process

1. Heat vegetable oil as well as switch the Ninja Speedi Rapid Cooker to the "Sauté" setting.
2. Add crushed garlic, ginger, as well as onion. Sauté onions until they are transparent.
3. Add the mutton pieces as well as brown them thoroughly.
4. Add tomatoes, sea salt, garam masala, cumin, turmeric, coriander, as well as coriander powder.
5. Choose "Pressure Cook" as well as cook for 20 Min.
6. Serve the mutton curry with rice or naan as well as garnish with diced cilantro..

Serving Total:

- Kcal:320
- Carbs: 12g
- Fat: 20g
- Protein: 26g

26. Speedy Lemon Garlic Shrimp Pasta

- Preparation Period: 15 Min
- Cooking Period: 15 Min
- Serves: 4

Ingredients needed:

- 1 lb. huge shrimp, stripped as well as deveined
- 8 oz linguine or spaghetti
- 2 tbsps.full of butter

- 3 cloves of garlic, crushed
- Zest as well as juice of 1 lemon
- 1/4 C. full of heavy cream
- 1/4 C. full of crushed Parmesan cheese
- Sea salt as well as black pepper as desired
- Fresh parsley for garnish

Preparation process

1. Follow the directions on the pasta package for cooking. Drain, then set apart.
2. Melt butter by using the "Sauté" setting on the Ninja Speedi Rapid Cooker.
3. Add the crushed garlic as well as cook it for one Min.
4. Add the shrimp as well as cook for 2 to 3 Min per side until pink.
5. Add the heavy cream, Parmesan cheese, lemon zest, as well as lemon juice.
6. Choose "Pressure Cook" as well as cook for 2 Min.
7. Over cooked pasta, top with the pasta as well as lemon garlic shrimp. Garnish with fresh parsley.

Serving Total:

- Kcal:400
- Carbs: 35g
- Fat: 15g
- Protein: 30g

27. Speedy Vegetarian Chickpea Curry

- Preparation Period: 15 Min
- Cooking Period: 20 Min
- Serves: 4

Ingredients needed:

- 2 cans (15 oz each) chickpeas, drained as well as rinsed
- 2 tbsps.full of vegetable oil
- 1 onion, diced
- 2 cloves of garlic, crushed
- 1-inch piece of ginger, crushed

- 2 tomatoes, diced
- 1 tbsp.full of curry powder
- 1 tsp. full of cumin
- 1 tsp. full of coriander
- 1/2 tsp. full of turmeric
- 1/2 tsp. full of Flakes of red pepper(adjust to taste)
- Sea salt as well as black pepper as desired
- 1/2 C. full of coconut milk
- Diced cilantro for garnish
- Cooked rice or naan for serving

Preparation process

1. Heat vegetable oil as well as switch the Ninja Speedi Rapid Cooker to the "Sauté" setting.
2. Add crushed garlic, ginger, as well as onion. Sauté onions until they are transparent.
3. Add the curry powder, cumin, coriander, turmeric, red pepper flakes, sea salt, as well as black pepper along with the diced tomatoes.
4. Add coconut milk as well as chickpeas. Stir thoroughly.
5. Choose "Pressure Cook" as well as cook for 10 Min.
6. Along with rice or naan, serve the chickpea curry with diced cilantro as a garnish.

Serving Total:

- Kcal:350
- Carbs: 40g
- Fat: 15g
- Protein: 15g

28. Speedy Pasta Primavera

- Preparation Period: 15 Min
- Cooking Period: 10 Min
- Serves: 4

Ingredients needed:

- 8 oz penne pasta
- 2 tbsps.full of olive oil
- 2 cloves of garlic, crushed
- 1 bell pepper, finely diced
- 1 zucchini, finely diced
- 1 C. full of cherry tomatoes, halved
- 1 C. full of broccoli florets
- 1/4 C. full of crushed Parmesan cheese
- Sea salt as well as black pepper as desired
- Fresh basil leaves for garnish

Preparation process

1. Follow the directions on the pasta package for cooking. Drain, then set apart.
2. Heat olive oil as well as use the "Sauté" setting in the Ninja Speedi Rapid Cooker.
3. Add the crushed garlic as well as cook it for one Min.
4. Add broccoli, bell pepper, zucchini, cherry tomatoes, as well as other ingredients. Cook for 3–4 Min.
5. Add the cooked pasta, Parmesan cheese that has been crumbled, sea salt, as well as black pepper.
6. Choose "Pressure Cook" as well as cook for 2 Min.
7. Serve the spaghetti primavera with fresh basil leaves as a garnish.

Serving Total:

- Kcal:350
- Carbs: 50g
- Fat: 10g
- Protein: 12g

- Preparation Period: 20 Min
- Cooking Period: 15 Min
- Serves: 6

Ingredients needed:

- 1 C. full of diced carrots
- 1 C. full of diced celery
- 1 onion, diced
- 2 cloves of garlic, crushed
- 1 can (15 oz) diced tomatoes
- 1 can (15 oz) kidney beans, drained as well as rinsed
- 1 C. full of green beans, diced
- 1 C. full of zucchini, diced
- 8 C. full of vegetable broth
- 1 C. full of small pasta
- 1 tsp. full of dried basil
- 1 tsp. full of dried oregano
- Sea salt as well as black pepper as desired
- Crushed Parmesan cheese for garnish

Preparation process

1. Choose "Sauté" in the Ninja Speedi Rapid Cooker as well as add diced onion, garlic, carrots, as well as celery. Sauté onions until they are transparent.
2. Along with spaghetti, dried basil, dried oregano, sea salt, as well as black pepper, add diced tomatoes, kidney beans, green beans, zucchini, as well as vegetable broth.
3. Choose "Pressure Cook" as well as cook for 10 Min.
4. Hot minestrone soup should be served with crushed Parmesan cheese on top.

Serving Total:

- Kcal:250
- Carbs: 45g
- Fat: 2g

- Protein: 10g

- Preparation Period: 20 Min
- Cooking Period: 15 Min
- Serves: 4

Ingredients needed:

- 1 lb. lamb chunks or skewers
- 2 tbsps.full of olive oil
- 2 cloves of garlic, crushed
- 1 tsp. full of cumin
- 1 tsp. full of paprika
- 1/2 tsp. full of coriander
- Sea salt as well as black pepper as desired
- Lemon wedges as well as tzatziki sauce for serving

Preparation process

1. Heat olive oil as well as use the "Sauté" setting in the Ninja Speedi Rapid Cooker.
2. Add the crushed garlic as well as cook it for one Min.
3. Add the cumin, paprika, coriander, sea salt, as well as black pepper along with the lamb chunks or skewers.
4. Cook the lamb for 3–4 Min per side, or until browned on all sides.
5. Add 5 more Min to the cooking time by choosing the "Pressure Cook" option.
6. Along with lemon wedges as well as tzatziki sauce, serve the lamb kebabs.

Serving Total:

- Kcal:300
- Carbs: 2g
- Fat: 20g
- Protein: 28g

- Preparation Period: 15 Min
- Cooking Period: 5 Min
- Serves: 4

Ingredients needed:

- 1 lb. huge shrimp, stripped as well as deveined
- 4 tbsps.full of butter
- 4 cloves of garlic, crushed
- Juice of 1 lemon
- 2 tbsps.full of diced fresh parsley
- Sea salt as well as black pepper as desired

Preparation process

1. In the Ninja Speedi Rapid Cooker, select the "Sauté" function as well as melt the butter.
2. Add crushed garlic as well as sauté for 1 Min.
3. Add shrimp as well as cook until pink, about 2 Min per side.
4. Stir in lemon juice, diced parsley, sea salt, as well as black pepper.
5. Serve the lemon garlic butter shrimp hot.

Serving Total:

- Kcal:250
- Carbs: 2g
- Fat: 18g
- Protein: 20g

32. Speedy Vegetarian Chili

- Preparation Period: 20 Min
- Cooking Period: 15 Min
- Serves: 6

Ingredients needed:

- 1 can (15 oz) black beans, drained as well as rinsed
- 1 can (15 oz) kidney beans, drained as well as rinsed
- 1 can (15 oz) diced tomatoes
- 1 C. full of corn kernels (fresh or frozen)
- 1 bell pepper, diced
- 1 onion, diced
- 2 cloves of garlic, crushed
- 2 tbsps.full of powdered chili
- 1 tsp. full of cumin
- Sea salt as well as black pepper as desired
- Sour cream as well as diced cheddar cheese for garnish

Preparation process

1. Select "Sauté" on the Ninja Speedi Rapid Cooker as well as add the diced bell pepper, onion, as well as garlic. Sauté onions until they are transparent.
2. Black beans, kidney beans, diced tomatoes, corn, cumin, sea salt, as well as black pepper should all be added.
3. Choose "Pressure Cook" as well as cook for 10 Min.
4. Serve the vegetarian chili hot with sour cream as well as cheddar cheese cubes as toppings.

Serving Total:

- Kcal:250
- Carbs: 48g
- Fat: 2g
- Protein: 10g

33. Speedy Tomato Basil Soup

- Preparation Period: 10 Min
- Cooking Period: 15 Min
- Serves: 4

Ingredients needed:

- 2 cans (28 oz each) of crushed tomatoes
- 2 C. full of vegetable broth
- 1/4 C. full of fresh basil leaves, diced
- 1/4 C. full of heavy cream
- 2 tbsps.full of olive oil
- 2 cloves of garlic, crushed
- Sea salt as well as black pepper as desired
- Crushed Parmesan cheese as well as fresh basil leaves for garnish

Preparation process

1. Heat olive oil as well as use the "Sauté" setting in the Ninja Speedi Rapid Cooker.
2. Add the crushed garlic as well as cook it for one Min.
3. Add the diced basil leaves, vegetable broth, as well as smashed tomatoes.
4. Choose "Pressure Cook" as well as cook for 10 Min.
5. Add black pepper, sea salt, as well as heavy cream by stirring.
6. Serve the tomato basil soup hot, topped with fresh basil leaves as well as Parmesan cheese that has been crushed.

Serving Total:

- Kcal:200
- Carbs: 20g
- Fat: 12g
- Protein: 4g

34. Speedy Chicken and Broccoli Alfredo

- Preparation Period: 15 Min
- Cooking Period: 10 Min
- Serves: 4

Ingredients needed:

- 1 lb. of chicken breasts without bones or skin, cut into bite-sized pieces.
- 2 tbsps.full of butter

- 2 cloves of garlic, crushed
- 2 C. full of broccoli florets
- 8 oz fettuccine pasta
- 1 C. full of heavy cream
- 1/2 C. full of crushed Parmesan cheese
- Sea salt as well as black pepper as desired
- Diced fresh parsley for garnish

Preparation process

1. Melt butter by using the "Sauté" setting on the Ninja Speedi Rapid Cooker.
2. Add the crushed garlic as well as cook it for one Min.
3. When the chicken is no longer pink, add it as well as simmer it.
4. After cooking for 2 more Min, stir in the broccoli florets.
5. Sea salt, black pepper, crumbled Parmesan cheese, as well as heavy cream should be added.
6. Choose "Pressure Cook" as well as cook for 3 Min.
7. Separately prepare the fettuccine spaghetti per the directions on the package, then combine with the chicken as well as broccoli mixture.
8. Hot Chicken as well as Broccoli Alfredo should be served with diced fresh parsley as a garnish.

Serving Total:

- Kcal:600
- Carbs: 45g
- Fat: 32g
- Protein: 35g

35. Speedy Beef Stroganoff

- Preparation Period: 15 Min
- Cooking Period: 10 Min
- Serves: 4

Ingredients needed:

- 1 lb. of beef sirloin, finely diced

- 2 tbsps.full of vegetable oil
- 1 onion, finely diced
- 2 cloves of garlic, crushed
- 8 oz mushrooms, diced
- 1 C. full of beef broth
- 1 tbsp.full of Worcestershire sauce
- 1/2 C. full of sour cream
- Sea salt as well as black pepper as desired
- Cooked egg noodles for serving
- Diced fresh parsley for garnish

Preparation process

1. Choose "Sauté" in the Ninja Speedi Rapid Cooker as well as warm some vegetable oil.
2. Add crushed garlic as well as diced onion. Sauté onions until they are transparent.
3. Cook the beef diced till browned after adding. Remove as well as reserve the beef.
4. Add diced mushrooms to the same cooker as well as cook for 2-3 Min.
5. Worcestershire sauce as well as beef broth are stirred in.
6. The beef should be placed back in the cooker as well as simmered for 2 Min.
7. Sour cream is added after the heat is turned off.
8. Over cooked egg noodles, top the beef stroganoff with diced fresh parsley.

Serving Total:

- Kcal:450
- Carbs: 20g
- Fat: 30g
- Protein: 25g

36. Speedy Shrimp Scampi

- Preparation Period: 10 Min
- Cooking Period: 5 Min
- Serves: 4

Ingredients needed:

- 1 lb. of huge shrimp, stripped as well as deveined
- 4 tbsps.full of butter
- 4 cloves of garlic, crushed
- Zest as well as juice of 1 lemon
- 1/4 C. full of white wine (optional)
- 2 tbsps.full of diced fresh parsley
- Sea salt as well as black pepper as desired
- Cooked linguine or spaghetti for serving

Preparation process

1. Melt butter by using the "Sauté" setting on the Ninja Speedi Rapid Cooker.
2. Add the crushed garlic as well as cook it for one Min.
3. Add the shrimp as well as cook for 2 Min on each side or until pink.
4. Add the lemon juice, zest, as well as white wine, if using, along with the parsley flakes as well as salt as well as pepper to taste.
5. Put the prepared spaghetti or linguine on top of the shrimp scampi.

Serving Total:

- Kcal:300
- Carbs: 20g
- Fat: 15g
- Protein: 20g

37. Speedy Vegetarian Stuffed Bell Peppers

- Preparation Period: 20 Min
- Cooking Period: 15 Min
- Serves: 4

Ingredients needed:

- 4 bell peppers, tops removed as well as seeds removed
- 1 C. full of cooked quinoa
- 1 can (15 oz) black beans, drained as well as rinsed

- 1 C. full of corn kernels (fresh or frozen)
- 1 C. full of diced tomatoes
- 1 C. full of diced cheddar cheese
- 1 tsp. full of powdered chili
- Sea salt as well as black pepper as desired
- Diced fresh cilantro for garnish

Preparation process

1. Choose the "Sauté" mode on the Ninja Speedi Rapid Cooker, then add the cooked quinoa, black beans, corn, diced tomatoes, chili powder, sea salt, as well as black pepper. For 5 Min, cook.
2. Sprinkle diced cheddar cheese on top after stuffing each bell pepper with the quinoa mixture.
3. Choose "Pressure Cook" as well as cook for 5 Min.
4. Warm vegetarian stuffed bell peppers should be served with fresh cilantro diced on top.

Serving Total:

- Kcal:350 kcal
- Carbs: 50g
- Fat: 12g
- Protein: 15g

38. Speedy Butternut Squash Soup

- Preparation Period: 15 Min
- Cooking Period: 15 Min
- Serves: 6

Ingredients needed:

- 1 butternut squash, stripped, seeded, as well as diced
- 1 onion, diced
- 2 cloves of garlic, crushed
- 4 C. full of vegetable broth
- 1 tsp. full of dried thyme

- Sea salt as well as black pepper as desired
- 1/2 C. full of heavy cream (optional)
- Roasted pumpkin seeds as well as fresh thyme for garnish

Preparation process

1. Select "Sauté" in the Ninja Speedi Rapid Cooker as well as add the crushed onion as well as garlic. Sauté onions until they are transparent.
2. Add the vegetable broth, dried thyme, sea salt, as well as black pepper along with the cubed butternut squash.
3. Choose "Pressure Cook" as well as cook for 10 Min.
4. Until the soup is creamy, purée it using an immersion blender. Alternately, pour the soup into a blender, puree it, as well as then put it back in the pot.
5. If using, stir in the heavy cream.
6. Warm butternut squash soup should be served with fresh thyme as well as roasted pumpkin seeds as garnishes.

Nutrition per Serving (without cream):

- Kcal:120 kcal
- Carbs: 30g
- Fat: 1g
- Protein: 2g

39. Speedy Thai Red Curry with Chicken

- Preparation Period: 20 Min
- Cooking Period: 10 Min
- Serves: 4

Ingredients needed:

- 1 lb. of Chicken thighs without bones as well as skin, cut into bite-sized pieces
- 2 tbsps.full of red curry paste
- 1 can (14 oz) of coconut milk
- 1 red bell pepper, diced
- 1 zucchini, diced
- 1 C. full of broccoli florets

- 1 tbsp.full of fish sauce
- 1 tbsp.full of brown sugar
- Lime wedges as well as fresh basil leaves for garnish
- Cooked jasmine rice for serving

Preparation process

1. In the Ninja Speedi Rapid Cooker, select the "Sauté" function as well as heat a tbsp.full of of oil.
2. Add chicken pieces as well as cook until browned. Remove as well as set aside.
3. In the same cooker, add red curry paste as well as sauté for 1 Min.
4. Pour in coconut milk, fish sauce, as well as brown sugar. Stir to combine.
5. Return the cooked chicken to the cooker, then add diced red bell pepper, zucchini, as well as broccoli.
6. Select the "Pressure Cook" function as well as cook for 3 Min.
7. Serve the Thai Red Curry with Chicken over jasmine rice, garnished with lime wedges as well as fresh basil leaves.

Serving Total:

- Kcal:450
- Carbs: 15g
- Fat: 30g
- Protein: 30g

40. Speedy Beef and Mushroom Risotto

- Preparation Period: 20 Min
- Cooking Period: 10 Min
- Serves: 4

Ingredients needed:

- 1 lb. of beef sirloin, finely diced
- 2 tbsps.full of olive oil
- 1 onion, finely diced
- 2 cloves of garlic, crushed
- 1 C. full of Arborio rice

- 8 oz of mushrooms, diced
- 1/2 C. full of dry white wine (optional)
- 4 C. full of beef broth, heated
- 1/2 C. full of crushed Parmesan cheese
- Sea salt as well as black pepper as desired
- Diced fresh parsley for garnish

Preparation process

1. Heat olive oil as well as use the "Sauté" setting in the Ninja Speedi Rapid Cooker.
2. Add crushed garlic as well as diced onion. Sauté onions until they are transparent.
3. For 3–4 Min, add the diced mushrooms as well as stir.
4. Cook Arborio rice for 1-2 Min after adding.
5. If using, add white wine as well as simmer until nearly evaporated.
6. Refill the cooker with the cooked beef.
7. One C. at a time, add heated beef broth gradually while continuously stirring until absorbed.
8. Add black pepper, sea salt, as well as crushed Parmesan cheese.
9. Choose "Pressure Cook" as well as cook for 5 Min.
10. Serve the heated Beef as well as Mushroom Risotto with diced fresh parsley as a garnish..

Serving Total:

- Kcal:450
- Carbs: 35g
- Fat: 20g
- Protein: 30g

Chapter 7:
Ninja Speedi Cooker Dinner Recipes

41. Ninja Speedi Rapid Cooker Teriyaki Pork Stir-Fry

- Preparation Period: 15 Min
- Cooking Period: 20 Min
- Serves: 4

Ingredients needed:

- 1 lb. pork tenderloin, finely diced
- 2 C. full of broccoli florets
- 1 red bell pepper, finely diced
- 1/2 C. full of diced carrots
- 1/4 C. full of low-sodium soy sauce
- 2 tbsps.full of honey
- 2 cloves of garlic, crushed
- 1 tbsp.full of sesame oil
- 1 tbsp.full of cornstarch
- 2 tbsps.full of water
- Cooked rice or noodles for serving

Preparation process

1. Combine soy sauce, honey, crushed garlic, as well as sesame oil in a bowl. Place aside.
2. Make a slurry of cornstarch as well as water in a separate small bowl.
3. Set the high heat setting on your Ninja Speedi Rapid Cooker to preheat.
4. Stir-fry the slices of pork until no longer pink. Take out of the cooker, then place aside.
5. To the cooker, add carrots, bell peppers, as well as broccoli. When they begin to soften, stir-fry.
6. Put the sauce mixture over the ingredients as well as add the pork back to the stove. Stir thoroughly.
7. As you stir the mixture, add the cornstarch slurry, as well as the sauce will thicken.
8. Over hot cooked rice or noodles, serve.

Serving Total:

- Kcal:320
- Carbs: 26g
- Fat: 9g
- Protein: 31g

42. Ninja Speedi Rapid Cooker Turkey Chili

- Preparation Period: 15 Min
- Cooking Period: 25 Min
- Serves: 6

Ingredients needed:

- 1 lb. crushed turkey
- 1 onion, diced
- 1 bell pepper, diced
- 2 cloves of garlic, crushed
- 1 can (15 oz) black beans, drained as well as rinsed
- 1 can (15 oz) diced tomatoes
- 1 C. full of frozen corn
- 2 tbsps.full of powdered chili

- 1 tsp. full of cumin
- Pepper as well as sea salt, as desired.
- Diced cheese as well as sour cream for garnish (optional)

Preparation process

1. Your Ninja Speedi Rapid Cooker should be set to the sauté setting.
2. Add the crumbled turkey as well as sauté, breaking it up as it browns.
3. Add the garlic, bell pepper, as well as onions. until softened, sauté.
4. Add the black beans, diced tomatoes, frozen corn, cumin, powdered chili, as well as salt & pepper to taste.
5. Then, set the pressure cooker for 10 Min on high pressure.
6. Five Min should pass naturally before you quickly remove any leftover pressure.
7. If preferred, top with sour cream as well as diced cheese when serving.

Serving Total:

- Kcal:280
- Carbs: 27g
- Fat: 8g
- Protein: 26g

43. Ninja Speedi Rapid Cooker Spicy Mutton Curry

- Preparation Period: 20 Min
- Cooking Period: 30 Min
- Serves: 4

Ingredients needed:

- 1 lb. of boneless mutton, cubed
- 1 onion, finely diced
- 2 tomatoes, diced
- 2 cloves of garlic, crushed
- 1-inch piece of ginger, crushed
- 2 tbsps.full of vegetable oil
- 2 tbsps.full of curry powder
- 1 tsp. full of cayenne pepper (adjust to taste)

- 1 C. full of coconut milk
- Sea salt to taste
- Fresh cilantro for garnish
- Cooked rice or naan bread for serving

Preparation process

1. Set the sauté setting on the Ninja Speedi Rapid Cooker.
2. Once the oil is hot, add the diced onions. till transparent, sauté.
3. Add the crushed garlic as well as ginger as well as continue to sauté for one more Min.
4. Add the mutton as well as stir; heat until browned all over.
5. Add sea salt, cayenne pepper, as well as curry powder. To evenly coat the meat, stir.
6. Cook the diced tomatoes until they are softened.
7. Place the lid on after adding the coconut milk. Put the cooker on a 15-Min pressure cook setting.
8. After five Min of natural pressure release, quickly relieve any leftover pressure.
9. Serve hot with rice or naan bread as well as fresh cilantro as a garnish.

Serving Total:

- Kcal:420
- Carbs: 12g
- Fat: 30g
- Protein: 30g

44. Ninja Speedi Rapid Cooker BBQ Pulled Pork

- Preparation Period: 15 Min
- Cooking Period: 45 Min
- Serves: 6

Ingredients needed:

- 3 lb.s pork shoulder, trimmed
- 1 C. full of BBQ sauce
- 1/2 C. full of apple cider vinegar

- 1/4 C. full of brown sugar
- 1 onion, diced
- 1 tsp. full of smoked paprika
- 1 tsp. full of garlic powder
- Pepper as well as sea salt, as desired.
- Hamburger buns for serving
- Coleslaw for topping (optional)

Preparation process

1. Your Ninja Speedi Rapid Cooker should be set to the sauté setting.
2. Garlic powder, smoked paprika, sea salt, as well as pepper are used to season the pork shoulder.
3. Add the pork shoulder to the cooker, then brown it on all sides.
4. Combine BBQ sauce, apple cider vinegar, as well as brown sugar in a separate bowl.
5. After adding diced onions, pour the sauce over the pork shoulder.
6. Then, set the pressure cooker for 30 Min on high pressure.
7. After 10 Min of natural pressure release, use two forks to julienne the pork.
8. If preferred, top the hamburger buns with coleslaw while serving the pulled pork.

Serving Total:

- Kcal:480 k
- Carbs: 32g
- Fat: 18g
- Protein: 40g

45. Ninja Speedi Rapid Cooker Turkey and Sweet Potato Stew

- Preparation Period: 20 Min
- Cooking Period: 25 Min
- Serves: 4

Ingredients needed:

- 1 lb. crushed turkey
- 2 sweet potatoes, stripped as well as cubed

- 1 onion, diced
- 2 cloves of garlic, crushed
- 4 C. full of chicken broth
- 1 can (15 oz) white beans, drained as well as rinsed
- 1 tsp. full of thyme
- Pepper as well as sea salt, as desired.
- Fresh parsley for garnish
- Crusty bread for serving

Preparation process

1. Set your Ninja Speedi Rapid Cooker to the sauté function.
2. Brown the crushed turkey, breaking it into crumbles.
3. Add diced onions as well as crushed garlic, sauté until softened.
4. Stir in sweet potatoes, chicken broth, white beans, thyme, sea salt, as well as pepper.
5. Close the lid as well as set the cooker to pressure cook for 15 Min.
6. Allow natural pressure release for 5 Min, then quick release the remaining pressure.
7. Serve hot, garnished with fresh parsley as well as with crusty bread on the side.

Serving Total:

- Kcal:340
- Carbs: 38g
- Fat: 7g
- Protein: 32g

46. Ninja Speedi Rapid Cooker Lemon Herb Pork Chops

- Preparation Period: 15 Min
- Cooking Period: 15 Min
- Serves: 4

Ingredients needed:

- 4 bone-in pork chops
- 2 lemons, zested as well as juiced

- 2 tbsps.full of olive oil
- 2 cloves of garlic, crushed
- 1 tsp. full of dried oregano
- 1 tsp. full of dried thyme
- Pepper as well as sea salt, as desired.
- Fresh parsley for garnish

Preparation process

1. Lemon zest, lemon juice, olive oil, smashed garlic, dried oregano, dried thyme, sea salt, as well as pepper should all be combined in a bowl.
2. The pork chops should marinate for at least 10 Min after being coated with the marinade.
3. Set the high heat setting on your Ninja Speedi Rapid Cooker to preheat.
4. Cook the marinated pork chops for 6-7 Min on each side, or until they reach an internal temperature of 145°F (63°C), in the cooker.
5. Serve hot with your preferred sides as well as garnish with fresh parsley.

Serving Total:

- Kcal:280
- Carbs: 4g
- Fat: 14g
- Protein: 32g

47. Ninja Speedi Rapid Cooker Moroccan Lamb Tagine

- Preparation Period: 20 Min
- Cooking Period: 30 Min
- Serves: 4

Ingredients needed:

- 1 lb. of boneless lamb, cubed
- 1 onion, finely diced
- 2 cloves of garlic, crushed
- 1 can (15 oz) diced tomatoes
- 1/2 C. full of dried apricots, diced

- 1/4 C. full of almonds, toasted
- 2 tsps. full of crushed cumin
- 2 tsps. full of crushed coriander
- 1 tsp. full of crushed cinnamon
- Pepper as well as sea salt, as desired.
- Fresh cilantro for garnish
- Cooked couscous for serving

Preparation process

1. Your Ninja Speedi Rapid Cooker should be set to the sauté setting.
2. Onion dice should be sautéed till transparent.
3. Sauté for another Min after adding the crushed garlic.
4. Lamb cubes are added, as well as it is browned all over.
5. Add the diced tomatoes, diced apricots, toasted almonds, cumin, coriander, as well as cinnamon, as well as the sea salt as well as pepper, as well as mix well.
6. Put the lid on the cooker as well as program it for 15 Min of pressure cooking.
7. After five Min of natural pressure release, quickly remove the remaining pressure.
8. Serve hot with fresh cilantro on top of cooked couscous.

Serving Total:

- Kcal:420
- Carbs: 28g
- Fat: 20g
- Protein: 32g

48. Lemon Herb Baked Salmon

- Preparation Period: 15 Min
- Cooking Period: 20 Min
- Serves: 4

Ingredients needed:

- 4 salmon fillets (6 oz each)
- 2 tbsps.full of olive oil
- 2 cloves of garlic, crushed

- 1 lemon, zested as well as juiced
- 1 tsp. full of dried oregano
- Pepper as well as sea salt, as desired.
- Fresh parsley for garnish

Preparation process

1. Your Ninja Speedi Rapid Cooker should be preheated to 375°F (190°C).
2. Olive oil, crushed garlic, lemon juice, zest, dried oregano, sea salt, as well as pepper should all be combined in a small bowl.
3. On the air-frying pan, arrange the salmon fillets as well as brush them with the lemon-herb mixture.
4. Cook the salmon for 20 Min, or until it is fully cooked as well as flaky.
5. Before serving, garnish with fresh parsley.

Serving Total

- Kcal:280
- Carbs: 2g
- Fat: 17g
- Protein: 29g

49. Crispy Air Fryer Chicken Tenders

- Preparation Period: 15 Min
- Cooking Period: 12 Min
- Serves: 4

Ingredients needed:

- 1 lb. of chicken tenders
- 1 C. full of panko breadcrumbs
- 1/2 C. full of crushed Parmesan cheese
- 1 tsp. full of paprika
- 1/2 tsp. full of garlic powder
- 2 eggs, beaten
- Cooking spray

Preparation process

1. Your Ninja Speedi Rapid Cooker should be preheated to 400°F (200°C).
2. Combine the panko breadcrumbs, crushed Parmesan, paprika, as well as garlic powder in a shallow dish.
3. Each chicken tender should be dipped into the beaten eggs before being coated in the breadcrumb mixture.
4. Spray some cooking spray on the air frying tray before adding the coated chicken tenders.
5. Cook the chicken for 12 Min, flipping it over halfway through, or until it is golden as well as crispy.

Serving Total

- Kcal:330
- Carbs: 14g
- Fat: 14g
- Protein: 35g

50. Vegan Chickpea and Spinach Curry

- Preparation Period: 15 Min
- Cooking Period: 15 Min
- Serves: 4

Ingredients needed:

- 2 cans (15 oz each) of chickpeas, drained as well as rinsed
- 1 onion, diced
- 2 cloves of garlic, crushed
- 1 can (14 oz) diced tomatoes
- 2 C. full of fresh spinach
- 1 can (14 oz) coconut milk
- 2 tbsps.full of curry powder
- Pepper as well as sea salt, as desired.
- Cooked rice or naan bread for serving

Preparation process

1. Your Ninja Speedi Rapid Cooker should be preheated to 350°F (175°C).
2. Diced onion as well as garlic should be sautéed in a pan until aromatic.
3. Curry powder, coconut milk, diced tomatoes, as well as chickpeas should all be added. Add pepper as well as sea salt for flavoring.
4. Stirring occasionally, add the ingredients to the saucepan of the Ninja Speedi Rapid Cooker. Cook for 15 Min.
5. Add the fresh spinach right before serving as well as toss until it wilts.
6. Serve with naan bread or over cooked rice.

Serving Total

- Kcal:390
- Carbs: 45g
- Fat: 18g
- Protein: 15g

51. Teriyaki Glazed Salmon Bowls

- Preparation Period: 20 Min
- Cooking Period: 15 Min
- Serves: 4

Ingredients needed:

- 4 salmon fillets (6 oz each)
- 1 C. full of cooked brown rice
- 2 C. full of broccoli florets
- 1/2 C. full of diced carrots
- 1/4 C. full of teriyaki sauce
- 2 tbsps.full of sesame seeds
- Green onions for garnish

Preparation process

1. Your Ninja Speedi Rapid Cooker should be preheated to 375°F (190°C).

2. Cook the broccoli as well as carrots in the air fryer for 10 Min, or until they are tender but still crisp.
3. Brush teriyaki sauce on the fish fillets while the vegetables are cooking.
4. Place the salmon fillets in the tray after removing the vegetables. Cook the fish for 15 Min, or until it is fully cooked.
5. Put cooked rice, fish, as well as steamed veggies in dishes.
6. Sesame seeds as well as green onions are used as garnish.

Serving Total

- Kcal:420 kcal
- Carbs: 30g
- Fat: 19g
- Protein: 32g

52. Vegan Spaghetti Aglio e Olio

- Preparation Period: 15 Min
- Cooking Period: 10 Min
- Serves: 4

Ingredients needed:

- 12 oz of spaghetti (use whole wheat for added fiber)
- 1/4 C. full of olive oil
- 4 cloves of garlic, finely diced
- 1/2 tsp. full of Flakes of red pepper(adjust to taste)
- Zest of 1 lemon
- Juice of 1 lemon
- Fresh parsley for garnish
- Pepper as well as sea salt, as desired.

Preparation process

1. Cook the spaghetti until al dente following the directions on the package. Drain, then set apart.
2. Your Ninja Speedi Rapid Cooker should be preheated to 350°F (175°C).

3. Heat the olive oil slowly in a saucepan. Red pepper flakes as well as crushed garlic are added. Garlic should be cooked until aromatic but not browned.
4. Toss the cooked spaghetti in the garlic-infused oil after adding it to the pan.
5. Lemon juice as well as zest have been added. As desired, add pepper as well as sea salt to the dish.
6. Before serving, garnish with fresh parsley.

Serving Total

- Kcal:320
- Carbs: 45g
- Fat: 14g
- Protein: 6g

53. Mongolian Beef

- Preparation Period: 20 Min
- Cooking Period: 10 Min
- Serves: 4

Ingredients needed:

- 1 lb. (450g) finely diced beef
- 1/4 C. full of cornstarch
- 3 tbsps.full of vegetable oil
- 2 cloves of garlic, crushed
- 1/2 C. full of low-sodium soy sauce
- 1/2 C. full of water
- 1/2 C. full of brown sugar
- 1/2 tsp. full of ginger, crushed
- Green onions, finely diced, for garnish

Preparation process

1. The beef dice should be thoroughly coated in cornstarch.
2. On the Ninja Speedi Rapid Cooker, choose "Sauté," then heat the vegetable oil.
3. Add the beef as well as heat it until it is browned as well as crispy. Remove as well as reserve the beef.

4. Ginger as well as garlic powder should be added to the same cooker. For around 30 seconds, sauté.
5. Add water, brown sugar, as well as soy sauce. Stirring is necessary to fully dissolve the sugar as well as slightly thicken the sauce.
6. Stir the cooked beef in the cooker one more to coat it with the sauce.
7. Add finely sliced green onions as a garnish.
8. Over cooked rice, please.

Serving Total

- Kcal:420
- Carbs: 41g
- Fat: 15g
- Protein: 30g

54. Korean Beef Bulgogi

- Preparation Period: 20 Min
- Cooking Period: 10 Min
- Serves: 4

Ingredients needed:

- 1 lb. (450g) finely diced beef
- 1/2 onion, finely diced
- 2 green onions, diced
- 3 cloves of garlic, crushed
- 1/4 C. full of soy sauce
- 2 tbsps.full of brown sugar
- 1 tbsp.full of sesame oil
- 1 tbsp.full of crushed ginger
- 1 tsp. full of sesame seeds
- 1/4 tsp. full of Flakes of red pepper(optional)

Preparation process

1. Combine soy sauce, brown sugar, sesame oil, diced ginger, sesame seeds, as well as red pepper flakes in a bowl (if using).

2. Combine the sauce mixture with the diced meat, onion, green onions, as well as smashed garlic. For at least 15 Min, marinate.
3. Heat the beef mixture using the "Sauté" setting on the Ninja Speedi Rapid Cooker. Cook the beef all the way through.
4. Serve hot in lettuce wraps or with steamed rice.

Serving Total:

- Kcal:320
- Carbs: 14g
- Fat: 14g
- Protein: 30g

55. Beef and Vegetable Soup

- Preparation Period: 20 Min
- Cooking Period: 25 Min
- Serves: 6

Ingredients needed:

- 1 lb. (450g) of beef stew meat, cubed
- 6 C. full of beef broth
- 2 carrots, diced
- 2 potatoes, diced
- 1 onion, diced
- 2 cloves of garlic, crushed
- 1 C. full of frozen peas
- Pepper as well as sea salt, as desired.
- Diced fresh parsley for garnish

Preparation process

1. Select the "Pressure Cook" function on the Ninja Speedi Rapid Cooker as well as add the beef cubes, beef broth, carrots, potatoes, onion, as well as crushed garlic. Season with sea salt as well as pepper.
2. Close the lid as well as set the cooker to high pressure for 15 Min.
3. Once the pressure cooking is done, release the pressure manually.

4. Open the lid, add the frozen peas, as well as simmer for another 5 Min.
5. Serve hot, garnished with diced fresh parsley.

Serving Total:

- Kcal:290
- Carbs: 24g
- Fat: 10g
- Protein: 25g

56. Beef Tacos

- Preparation Period: 15 Min
- Cooking Period: 10 Min
- Serves: 4

Ingredients needed:

- 1 lb. (450g) of crushed beef
- 1 packet taco seasoning mix
- 1/2 C. full of water
- 1 C. full of diced lettuce
- 1 C. full of diced tomatoes
- 1/2 C. full of diced cheddar cheese
- 1/4 C. full of diced onions
- 1/4 C. full of sour cream
- 8 small taco shells

Preparation process

1. In the Ninja Speedi Rapid Cooker, select the "Sauté" function as well as cook the crushed beef until browned. Drain any excess fat.
2. Add the taco seasoning mix as well as water. Stir as well as simmer until the mixture thickens.
3. Warm the taco shells in the cooker using the "Steam" function for a Min or two.
4. Assemble the tacos: Spoon the beef mixture into each taco shell, as well as top with lettuce, tomatoes, diced cheddar cheese, diced onions, as well as sour cream.
5. Serve immediately.

Serving Total:

- Kcal:380 kcal
- Carbs: 18g
- Fat: 25g
- Protein: 20g

57. Beef and Cheese Quesadillas

- Preparation Period: 10 Min
- Cooking Period: 10 Min
- Serves: 4

Ingredients needed:

- 1 lb. (450g) of finely diced beef
- 1 C. full of diced cheddar cheese
- 4 huge flour tortillas
- 1/2 C. full of diced tomatoes
- 1/4 C. full of diced green bell pepper
- 1/4 C. full of diced red onion
- 1/4 C. full of diced fresh cilantro
- 1/4 C. full of sour cream
- Salsa for dipping (optional)

Preparation process

1. Choose the "Sauté" mode on the Ninja Speedi Rapid Cooker, as well as cook the diced beef there until browned. Remove as well as reserve the beef.
2. Sprinkle cheddar cheese dice over one tortilla before placing it in the cooker.
3. On one side of the tortilla, place diced tomatoes, diced green bell pepper, diced red onion, as well as diced cilantro along with the cooked meat.
4. To form a half-moon, fold the remaining tortilla over the filling.
5. Gently press down with a spatula as well as heat, flipping halfway through, until the tortilla is crispy as well as the cheese is melted.
6. the remaining tortillas, as well as repeat.
7. If desired, cut the quesadillas into wedges as well as serve with salsa as well as sour cream for dipping.

Serving Total:

- Kcal:480
- Carbs: 28g
- Fat: 28g
- Protein: 30g

58. Beef and Peppers Stir-Fry

- Preparation Period: 15 Min
- Cooking Period: 10 Min
- Serves: 4

Ingredients needed:

- 1 lb. (450g) finely diced beef
- 2 tbsps.full of vegetable oil
- 1 onion, finely diced
- 1 red bell pepper, finely diced
- 1 green bell pepper, finely diced
- 1 C. full of snap peas or snow peas
- 3 cloves of garlic, crushed
- 1/4 C. full of soy sauce
- 2 tbsps.full of hoisin sauce
- 1 tbsp.full of brown sugar
- 1 tsp. full of cornstarch mixed with 2 tbsps.full of water
- Sesame seeds as well as diced green onions for garnish

Preparation process

1. Heat the vegetable oil in the Sauté setting of the Ninja Speedi Rapid Cooker.
2. Cook the beef diced till browned after adding. Remove as well as reserve the beef.
3. Snap peas, red as well as green bell peppers, diced onion, as well as crushed garlic are all added to the same cooker. For 3–4 Min, sauté until just barely tender.
4. Combine the cornstarch mixture, soy sauce, hoisin sauce, brown sugar, as well as in a small bowl.
5. Bring the cooked beef back to the cooker, cover with the sauce, as well as stir-fry for an additional two to three Min until the sauce has thickened.

6. Sesame seeds as well as green onion dice can be used as a garnish.
7. Serve warm alongside steaming rice.

Serving Total:

- Carbs: 18g
- Fat: 14g
- Protein: 30g
- Kcal:350

59. Beef and Mushroom Risotto

- Preparation Period: 15 Min
- Cooking Period: 20 Min
- Serves: 4

Ingredients needed:

- 1 lb. (450g) beef sirloin, finely diced
- 2 tbsps.full of olive oil
- 1 onion, finely diced
- 2 cloves of garlic, crushed
- 1 C. full of Arborio rice
- 1/2 C. full of dry white wine (optional)
- 4 C. full of beef broth, heated
- 8 oz (225g) mushrooms, diced
- 1/2 C. full of crushed Parmesan cheese
- Pepper as well as sea salt, as desired.
- Fresh parsley for garnish

Preparation process

1. Heat the olive oil on the "Sauté" setting of the Ninja Speedi Rapid Cooker.
2. Cook the beef diced till browned after adding. Remove as well as reserve the beef.
3. Add crushed garlic as well as diced onion to the same cooker. Sauté the onion until it turns translucent.
4. Arborio rice should be cooked for 1-2 Min, until it is just beginning to toast.
5. White wine should be added if using, then cooked until mostly absorbed.

6. One ladle at a time, start adding the heated beef broth. Stir continuously as well as wait until the liquid has been absorbed before adding more. Continue cooking the rice until it is creamy as well as the desired softness (usually about 18-20 Min).
7. Add the diced mushrooms as well as keep stirring throughout the final five Min of simmering.
8. Crushed Parmesan cheese is added to the cooked beef when it is returned to the cooker. The mixture is then stirred until creamy.
9. As desired, add pepper as well as sea salt to the dish.
10. Serve hot as well as garnish with fresh parsley.

Serving Total:

- Kcal:490
- Carbs: 45g
- Fat: 20g
- Protein: 30g

60. Beef and Potato Curry

- Preparation Period: 20 Min
- Cooking Period: 25 Min
- Serves: 4

Ingredients needed:

- 1 lb. (450g) of stewing beef, cubed
- 2 tbsps.full of vegetable oil
- 1 onion, finely diced
- 2 cloves of garlic, crushed
- 1 tbsp.full of curry powder
- 1 tsp. full of crushed cumin
- 1 tsp. full of crushed coriander
- 1/2 tsp. full of crushed turmeric
- 1 can (14 oz) of diced tomatoes
- 2 C. full of diced potatoes
- 1 C. full of beef broth
- 1/2 C. full of coconut milk
- Pepper as well as sea salt, as desired.

- Diced fresh cilantro for garnish
- Cooked rice for serving

Preparation process

1. Heat the vegetable oil in the Sauté setting of the Ninja Speedi Rapid Cooker.
2. Cook the meat cubes until browned after adding them. Remove as well as reserve the beef.
3. Add crushed garlic as well as diced onion to the same cooker. The onion should be cooked until tender as well as transparent.
4. Add the curry powder, turmeric, as well as the crushed cumin, coriander, as well as coriander. Cook until aromatic for 1-2 Min.
5. Add the beef broth, coconut milk, diced tomatoes, as well as diced potatoes. Stir thoroughly.
6. Select the "Pressure Cook" setting, add the cooked meat back to the cooker, as well as secure the lid. For 15 Min, place the cooker under high pressure.
7. Once the food has finished cooking under pressure, manually release the pressure.
8. As desired, add pepper as well as sea salt to the dish.
9. Serve immediately over hot rice as well as top with fresh cilantro dice as a garnish.

Serving Total:

- Kcal:520
- Carbs: 33g
- Fat: 26g
- Protein: 38g

Chapter 8:
Ninja Speedi Cooker Dessert Recipes

61. Chocolate Lava Cake

- Preparation Period: 10 Min
- Cooking Period: 15 Min
- Serves: 4

Ingredients needed:

- 1/2 C. full of semi-sweet chocolate chips
- 1/4 C. full of unsea salted butter
- 1/4 C. full of granulated sugar
- 2 huge eggs
- 2 tbsps.full of all-purpose flour
- 1/2 tsp. full of vanilla extract
- Pinch of sea salt
- Powdered sugar for dusting

Preparation process

1. Put butter as well as chocolate chips in the Ninja Speedi Cooker pot. Sauté the food in the cooker while stirring until it is smooth as well as melted.

2. When the mixture is thoroughly blended, turn off the heat as well as whisk in the sugar, eggs, flour, vanilla essence, as well as a small amount of sea salt.
3. The batter should be poured into buttered ramekins before being foil-wrapped.
4. The steam rack should be placed inside the Speedi Cooker after adding 1 C. worth of water to the bottom. Put the ramekins in a row on the rack.
5. The cakes should be cooked until they are set at the edges but remain oozy in the center, then secure the lid as well as choose the Steam option for 15 Min.
6. Remove the ramekins with care, sprinkle with confectioners' sugar, as well as serve right away.

Serving Total

- Kcal:350
- Carbs: 30g
- Fat: 22g
- Protein: 4g

---

62. Berry Cobbler

- Preparation Period: 15 Min
- Cooking Period: 30 Min
- Serves: 6

Ingredients needed:

- 3 C. full of mixed berries (strawberries, blueberries, raspberries)
- 1/2 C. full of granulated sugar
- 1 C. full of all-purpose flour
- 1 C. full of milk
- 1/4 C. full of unsea salted butter
- 1 tsp. full of vanilla extract
- 1/2 tsp. full of baking powder
- Pinch of sea salt
- Vanilla ice cream (optional)

Preparation process

1. In the Ninja Speedi Cooker pot, add 1/4 cup of sugar as well as the mixed berries. Cook the berries in the Sauté setting until they start to release their juices as well as soften. Get rid of the heat.
2. The flour, remaining sugar, milk, melted butter, vanilla extract, baking powder, as well as a dash of sea salt should all be combined in a another basin as well as whisked until smooth.
3. Over the cooked berries in the pot, pour the batter.
4. The cobbler should be golden brown as well as bubbling after 30 Min of baking in the Speedi Cooker's Bake mode at 350°F.
5. If desired, serve warm with a scoop of vanilla ice cream.

Serving Total

- Kcal:290
- Carbs: 52g
- Fat: 7g
- Protein: 4g

63. Lemon Bars

- Preparation Period: 15 Min
- Cooking Period: 25 Min
- Serves: 9

Ingredients needed:

- 1 C. full of all-purpose flour
- 1/2 C. full of powdered sugar
- 1/2 C. full of unsea salted butter, cold as well as cubed
- 2 huge eggs
- 1 C. full of granulated sugar
- 2 tbsps.full of all-purpose flour
- 2 tbsps.full of lemon juice
- Zest of 1 lemon
- 1/4 tsp. full of baking powder
- Powdered sugar for dusting

Preparation process

1. Combine 1 C. of flour, 1 C. of powdered sugar, as well as 1 C. of chilled butter in a food processor. Pulse the ingredients only until it resembles coarse crumbs.
2. To create the crust, press the mixture into the bottom of a greased Ninja Speedi Cooker pot.
3. The crust should be faintly brown after 15 Min of baking in the Speedi Cooker at 350°F.
4. Lemon juice, lemon zest, baking powder, 2 tablespoons of flour, as well as eggs should all be thoroughly blended in a bowl.
5. Over the baked crust, pour the lemon mixture.
6. The lemon bars should be firm as well as the edges brown after 25 Min of baking at 350°F with the lid on.
7. Let them cool before cutting them into squares as well as dusted with powdered sugar.

Serving Total

- Kcal:260
- Carbs: 39g
- Fat: 11g
- Protein: 3g

64. Rice Pudding

- Preparation Period: 10 Min
- Cooking Period: 20 Min
- Serves: 4

Ingredients needed:

- 1/2 C. full of Arborio rice
- 4 C. full of milk
- 1/2 C. full of granulated sugar
- 1 tsp. full of vanilla extract
- 1/2 tsp. full of crushed cinnamon
- 1/4 tsp. full of sea salt
- Raisins as well as crushed nutmeg for garnish (optional)

Preparation process

1. In the Ninja Speedi Cooker pot, combine the rice, milk, sugar, vanilla extract, crushed cinnamon, as well as sea salt.
2. Put the Speedi Cooker in pressure mode for 20 Min, then close the lid.
3. Once the food is finished cooking, manually release the pressure before cautiously opening the lid.
4. Rice pudding should be stirred before adding some raisins for sweetness, if desired.
5. Rice pudding can be served warm, cold, or chilled. Crushed nutmeg should be used as a garnish.

Serving Total

- Kcal:350
- Carbs: 61g
- Fat: 7g
- Protein: 8g

65. Apple Crisp

- Preparation Period: 15 Min
- Cooking Period: 30 Min
- Serves: 6

Ingredients needed:

- 4 C. full of diced apples (stripped as well as cored)
- 1 tbsp.full of lemon juice
- 1/2 C. full of granulated sugar
- 1/2 tsp. full of crushed cinnamon
- 1/4 tsp. full of crushed nutmeg
- 1/2 C. full of old-fashioned oats
- 1/4 C. full of all-purpose flour
- 1/4 C. full of brown sugar
- 1/4 C. full of unsea salted butter, melted
- Vanilla ice cream (optional)

Preparation process

1. In a bowl, toss the diced apples with lemon juice, granulated sugar, crushed cinnamon, as well as crushed nutmeg.
2. Transfer the apple mixture to the Ninja Speedi Cooker pot.
3. In another bowl, combine oats, flour, brown sugar, as well as melted butter. Mix until crumbly.
4. Sprinkle the oat mixture evenly over the apples in the pot.
5. Close the lid as well as set the Speedi Cooker to Bake mode at 375°F for 30 Min or until the topping is golden as well as the apples are bubbling.
6. Serve the apple crisp warm, as well as if you like, top it with a scoop of vanilla ice cream.

Serving Total

- Kcal:290
- Carbs: 58g
- Fat: 6g
- Protein: 2g

66. Chocolate Peanut Butter Mug Cake

- Preparation Period: 5 Min
- Cooking Period: 2 Min
- Serves: 1

Ingredients needed:

- 3 tbsps.full of all-purpose flour
- 2 tbsps.full of granulated sugar
- 1 1/2 tbsps.full of unsweetened cocoa powder
- 1/4 tsp. full of baking powder
- A pinch of sea salt
- 2 tbsps.full of milk
- 1 1/2 tbsps.full of creamy peanut butter
- 1/2 tsp. full of vanilla extract
- 1 tbsp.full of semi-sweet chocolate chips

Preparation process

1. Combine the flour, sugar, baking powder, cocoa powder, as well as a dash of sea salt in a cup that is microwave-safe.
2. The mug should now contain milk, peanut butter, as well as vanilla essence. When the batter is smooth as well as thoroughly incorporated, stir.
3. The batter is covered with chocolate chunks.
4. Close the cover on the Ninja Speedi Cooker after placing the mug inside.
5. When the cake has risen as well as feels firm to the touch, set the Speedi Cooker to the microwave setting for 2 Min.
6. Enjoy your warm as well as gooey chocolate peanut butter mug cake after carefully removing the mug (it will be hot).

Serving Total

- Kcal:420
- Carbs: 62g
- Fat: 16g
- Protein: 10g

67. Caramelized Banana Foster

- Preparation Period: 10 Min
- Cooking Period: 15 Min
- Serves: 4

Ingredients needed:

- 4 ripe bananas, diced
- 1/2 C. full of brown sugar
- 1/4 C. full of unsea salted butter
- 1/4 C. full of dark rum
- 1 tsp. full of crushed cinnamon
- Vanilla ice cream (optional)
- Diced pecans for garnish (optional)

Preparation process

1. Melt the butter in the Ninja Speedi Cooker pot on the Sauté setting.
2. Brown sugar as well as cinnamon are added to the melted butter, as well as the mixture is stirred until the sugar is dissolved as well as the mixture turns frothy as well as caramelized.
3. Pour the black rum in slowly as well as simmer for another Min while stirring to let the alcohol burn off.
4. Bananas should be added to the pot as well as gently mixed into the caramel sauce.
5. Once the bananas are softened as well as covered with the caramel sauce, close the top as well as continue cooking them in the Sauté mode on the Speedi Cooker for an extra 5 Min.
6. If serving warm, top vanilla ice cream with the banana foster as well as top with diced nuts for more crunch as well as taste.

Serving Total

- Kcal:280
- Carbs: 51g
- Fat: 8g
- Protein: 1g

68. Mixed Berry Crisp

- Preparation Period: 15 Min
- Cooking Period: 35 Min
- Serves: 6

Ingredients needed:

- 4 C. full of mixed berries (strawberries, blueberries, raspberries)
- 1/2 C. full of granulated sugar
- 1 tbsp.full of cornstarch
- 1 tsp. full of lemon juice
- 1 C. full of old-fashioned oats
- 1/2 C. full of all-purpose flour
- 1/2 C. full of brown sugar
- 1/2 tsp. full of crushed cinnamon

- 1/4 tsp. full of sea salt
- 1/2 C. full of unsea salted butter, melted
- Vanilla ice cream or whipped cream for serving (optional)

Preparation process

1. The mixed berries, cornstarch, lemon juice, as well as granulated sugar should all be combined in a sizable basin. Transfer the mixture to the Ninja Speedi Cooker pot after tossing until the berries are thoroughly covered.
2. Combine the oats, flour, brown sugar, crushed cinnamon, as well as sea salt in the same bowl. Melted butter should be added, then the mixture should be stirred up into a crumbly topping.
3. The berries in the pot will be equally covered with the oat mixture.
4. Turn the Speedi Cooker to Bake mode as well as set the temperature to 375°F for 35 Min, or until the topping is golden brown as well as the berries are bubbling. Close the lid.
5. Before serving, let the berry crisp cool just a little.
6. Serve warm, perhaps garnished with a dollop of whipped cream or a scoop of vanilla ice cream.

Serving Total

- Kcal:350
- Carbs: 58g
- Fat: 13g
- Protein: 3g

69. Pumpkin Spice Bread Pudding

- Preparation Period: 15 Min
- Cooking Period: 25 Min
- Serves: 6

Ingredients needed:

- 4 C. full of cubed day-old bread (such as French or Italian)
- 1 C. full of canned pumpkin puree
- 3/4 C. full of granulated sugar
- 2 huge eggs

- 1 C. full of milk
- 1 tsp. full of vanilla extract
- 1 tsp. full of crushed cinnamon
- 1/2 tsp. full of crushed nutmeg
- 1/4 tsp. full of crushed cloves
- 1/4 tsp. full of sea salt
- Whipped cream or vanilla sauce for serving (optional)

Preparation process

1. Pumpkin puree, granulated sugar, eggs, milk, vanilla essence, crushed cinnamon, crushed nutmeg, crushed cloves, as well as sea salt should all be thoroughly blended in a large basin.
2. Cubed bread should be added to the bowl as well as gently tossed to uniformly distribute the pumpkin mixture on the bread. Allow the bread to absorb the liquid for about 10 Min.
3. Insert the Ninja Speedi Cooker pot with the bread as well as pumpkin mixture.
4. Turn the Speedi Cooker to Bake mode as well as set the temperature to 350°F for 25 Min, or until the pudding is set as well as the top is golden brown. Close the lid.
5. Before serving, let the bread pudding cool just a little.
6. For an extra sweet touch, serve with a dollop of whipped cream or a drizzle of vanilla sauce.

Serving Total

- Kcal:280
- Carbs: 54g
- Fat: 5g
- Protein: 7g

70. Tiramisu Parfait

- Preparation Period: 20 Min
- Chilling Period: 2 hours
- Serves: 4

Ingredients needed:

- 1 C. full of mascarpone cheese
- 1/2 C. full of heavy cream
- 1/2 C. full of strong brewed coffee, cooled
- 2 tbsps.full of coffee liqueur (optional)
- 1/2 C. full of powdered sugar
- 1 tsp. full of vanilla extract
- 8 ladyfinger cookies, broken into pieces
- Cocoa powder for dusting
- Chocolate shavings for garnish (optional)

Preparation process

1. Mascarpone cheese, heavy cream, confectioners' sugar, as well as vanilla essence should all be combined in a bowl. Whip the ingredients until firm peaks form as well as it is smooth.
2. Coffee liqueur, if using, as well as the cooled, brewed coffee should be combined in a separate bowl.
3. The dessert should be layered in serving glasses or jars. Each glass should first have a layer of ladyfinger pieces at the bottom.
4. Over the ladyfingers, spoon a layer of the mascarpone mixture.
5. Over the mascarpone top, drizzle a little of the coffee mixture.
6. The layers are repeated until the glasses are full, as well as then a layer of mascarpone is placed on top.
7. Refrigerate the glasses for at least two hours to enable the flavors to mingle. Cover the glasses with plastic wrap.
8. Dust the tops with cocoa powder before serving as well as, if preferred, cover with chocolate shavings.

Serving Total

- Kcal:450
- Carbs: 28g
- Fat: 31g
- Protein: 7g

- Preparation Period: 10 Min
- Cooking Period: 20 Min
- Chilling Period: 2 hours
- Serves: 4

Ingredients needed:

- 1 C. full of Arborio rice
- 2 C. full of coconut milk
- 2 C. full of whole milk
- 1/2 C. full of granulated sugar
- 1 ripe mango, stripped, pitted, as well as diced
- 1/2 tsp. full of vanilla extract
- 1/4 tsp. full of crushed cardamom (optional)
- Toasted coconut flakes for garnish (optional)

Preparation process

1. Drain after giving the Arborio rice a cold water rinse.
2. Combine the coconut milk, full milk, as well as rice that has been washed in the Ninja Speedi Cooker pot.
3. Put the Speedi Cooker in the Pressure setting for 8 Min, then close the cover.
4. Once the food is finished cooking, manually release the pressure before cautiously opening the lid.
5. Add the granulated sugar, mango cubes, vanilla extract, as well as cardamom seeds (if using). Mix thoroughly.
6. When the rice pudding has cooled to room temperature, place it in the refrigerator as well as chill for at least two hours.
7. If desired, top each bowl of the mango coconut rice pudding with toasted coconut flakes.

Serving Total

- Kcal:450
- Carbs: 70g
- Fat: 16g

- Protein: 5g

- Preparation Period: 10 Min
- Cooking Period: 10 Min
- Serves: 4

Ingredients needed:

- 1 C. full of heavy cream
- 1 C. full of semi-sweet chocolate chips
- 1/2 C. full of creamy peanut butter
- 1/4 C. full of powdered sugar
- 1 tsp. full of vanilla extract
- Assorted dippers: strawberries, banana slices, marshmallows, pretzel sticks, as well as cubed lb. cake

Preparation process

1. Heat the heavy cream in the Ninja Speedi Cooker pot on the Sauté setting until it begins to simmer.
2. Add the powdered sugar, vanilla extract, creamy peanut butter, as well as chocolate chips after lowering the heat to low.
3. As soon as the chocolate as well as peanut butter are fully melted as well as the mixture is shiny as well as smooth, continue stirring.
4. Depending on your preference, either pour the fondue into a serving bowl or leave it in the Speedi Cooker pot.
5. The fondue should be served right away with a variety of dippers for a delightful as well as entertaining dessert.

Serving Total
- Kcal:480
- Carbs: 31g
- Fat: 36g
- Protein: 8g

- Preparation Period: 15 Min
- Cooking Period: 15 Min
- Chilling Period: 2 hours
- Serves: 6

Ingredients needed:

- 1 1/2 C. full of graham cracker crumbs
- 1/2 C. full of unsea salted butter, melted
- 1/4 C. full of granulated sugar
- 1 can (14 Oz.) of sweetened condensed milk
- 3/4 C. full of fresh key lime juice (or regular lime juice)
- Zest of 2 key limes (or regular limes)
- 2 huge eggs
- Whipped cream as well as lime slices for garnish (optional)

Preparation process

1. Granulated sugar, melted butter, as well as graham cracker crumbs should all be combined in a bowl. Mix just enough to coat the crumbs all over.
2. To make the pie crust layer, press the crumb mixture into the bottom of serving glasses or jars.
3. Eggs, sweetened condensed milk, fresh lime juice, as well as lime zest should all be thoroughly blended in a different bowl.
4. For each glass, add the lime mixture on top of the crust.
5. Put the glasses in the pot of the Ninja Speedi Cooker. Fill the bottom of the Speedi Cooker with 1 C. of water.
6. When the pie filling is set, close the cover as well as use the Speedi Cooker's Bake mode in the oven at 350°F for 15 Min.
7. The glasses should be taken out of the Speedi Cooker as well as let to cool to room temperature.
8. To chill as well as set, refrigerate the Key Lime Pie C. full of for at least two hours.
9. If you'd like, top the dish off with some whipped cream as well as a lime slice before serving.

Serving Total

- Kcal:420
- Carbs: 51g
- Fat: 21g
- Protein: 8g

74. Raspberry White Chocolate Bread Pudding

- Preparation Period: 15 Min
- Cooking Period: 35 Min
- Serves: 6

Ingredients needed:

- 4 C. full of cubed day-old bread (such as French or Italian)
- 1 C. full of fresh raspberries
- 1/2 C. full of white chocolate chips
- 1 C. full of whole milk
- 1 C. full of heavy cream
- 3/4 C. full of granulated sugar
- 2 huge eggs
- 1 tsp. full of vanilla extract
- 1/4 tsp. full of almond extract (optional)
- Powdered sugar for dusting

Preparation process

1. Whole milk, heavy cream, sugar, eggs, vanilla extract, as well as almond extract (if using) should all be thoroughly blended in a bowl.
2. In the Ninja Speedi Cooker pot, add the cubed bread, fresh raspberries, as well as white chocolate chips.
3. In order to uniformly coat the bread as well as spread the raspberries as well as chocolate chips, pour the milk mixture over the bread as well as gently toss.
4. Turn the Speedi Cooker to Bake mode as well as set the temperature to 350°F for 35 Min, or until the bread pudding is set as well as the top is golden.
5. Before serving, let the bread pudding cool for a few Min.

6. Just before serving, sprinkle powdered sugar over the top for a refined appearance.

Serving Total

- Kcal:480
- Carbs: 59g
- Fat: 24g
- Protein: 10g

75. Chocolate-Dipped Strawberries

- Preparation Period: 10 Min
- Cooking Period: 5 Min
- Chilling Period: 30 Min
- Serves: 4

Ingredients needed:

- 16 fresh strawberries, washed as well as dried
- 1 C. full of semi-sweet chocolate chips
- 2 tbsps.full of heavy cream
- 1/4 C. full of diced nuts (e.g., almonds, pistachios) or sprinkles (optional)

Preparation process

1. Add the heavy cream as well as chocolate chips to the Ninja Speedi Cooker pot.
2. Once the chocolate is all melted as well as smooth, switch the Speedi Cooker to Sauté mode as well as keep stirring. Get rid of the heat.
3. Each strawberry should be dipped into the melted chocolate as well as coated about halfway. All extra chocolate should drip off.
4. Put the chocolate-covered strawberries on a tray covered with parchment paper.
5. Add diced nuts or vibrant sprinkles to the wet chocolate as desired.
6. To allow the chocolate to set, chill the strawberries in the refrigerator for at least 30 Min.
7. Serve the chocolate-covered strawberries as a lovely as well as classy dessert once the chocolate has hardened.

Serving Total

- Kcal:220 kcal
- Carbs: 25g
- Fat: 13g
- Protein: 2g

76. Coconut Mango Rice Pudding

- Preparation Period: 15 Min
- Cooking Period: 20 Min
- Chilling Period: 2 hours
- Serves: 4

Ingredients needed:

- 1 C. full of Arborio rice
- 1 1/2 C. full of coconut milk
- 1 1/2 C. full of whole milk
- 1/2 C. full of granulated sugar
- 1 ripe mango, stripped, pitted, as well as diced
- 1/4 C. full of diced coconut (toasted for garnish, if desired)
- 1/2 tsp. full of vanilla extract
- A pinch of sea salt

Preparation process

1. Drain after giving the Arborio rice a cold water rinse.
2. Combine the coconut milk, full milk, as well as rice that has been washed in the Ninja Speedi Cooker pot.
3. Put the Speedi Cooker in the Pressure setting for 8 Min, then close the cover.
4. Once the food is finished cooking, manually release the pressure before cautiously opening the lid.
5. Add a dash of sea salt along with the granulated sugar, diced mango, vanilla extract, as well as diced coconut (if using). Mix thoroughly.
6. Let the coconut mango rice pudding come to room temperature before chilling as well as setting it in the refrigerator for at least two hours.

7. If preferred, top each bowl of the dessert with toasted diced coconut as well as more mango chunks.

Serving Total

- Kcal:400
- Carbs: 75g
- Fat: 8g
- Protein: 6g

77. Nutella-Stuffed Crepes

- Preparation Period: 15 Min
- Cooking Period: 15 Min
- Serves: 4

Ingredients needed:

For the Crepes:

- 1 C. full of all-purpose flour
- 2 huge eggs
- 1 1/4 C. full of milk
- 2 tbsps.full of unsea salted butter, melted
- 1 tbsp.full of granulated sugar
- 1/2 tsp. full of vanilla extract
- A pinch of sea salt

For the Filling:

- 1/2 C. full of Nutella or chocolate hazelnut spread
- Diced bananas, strawberries, or raspberries (optional)
- Powdered sugar for dusting
- Whipped cream for topping (optional)

Preparation process

1. The flour, eggs, milk, melted butter, granulated sugar, vanilla essence, as well as a dash of sea salt should all be combined in a blender. Blend the batter up to smoothness.
2. On Sauté mode, preheat the Ninja Speedi Cooker. Add a little butter or oil to the surface to give it a light coating.
3. A tiny amount of crepe batter should be poured into the Speedi Cooker, as well as it should be swirled around to evenly cover the bottom. Cook for about 1-2 Min, or until the bottom turns golden brown as well as the edges begin to lift.
4. Use a spatula to carefully turn the crepe, then cook the opposite side for an additional one to two Min. Stacking the cooked crepes on a plate, repeat this procedure until all the batter has been utilized.
5. Each crepe should be smeared with Nutella or chocolate hazelnut spread.
6. If desired, incorporate diced strawberries, bananas, or berries.
7. The crepes should be rolled up as well as placed in the Ninja Speedi Cooker for a Min to stay heated.
8. Warm Nutella-Stuffed Crepes should be served with powdered sugar on top.
9. For an extra decadent treat, top with whipped cream.

Nutrition (per serving, without toppings):

- Kcal:350
- Carbs: 43g
- Fat: 16g
- Protein: 9g

78. Cherry Almond Clafoutis

- Preparation Period: 15 Min
- Cooking Period: 25 Min
- Serves: 6

Ingredients needed:

- 1 C. full of fresh or frozen pitted cherries
- 3/4 C. full of whole milk
- 1/2 C. full of granulated sugar

- 3 huge eggs
- 1/2 C. full of all-purpose flour
- 1/2 tsp. full of almond extract
- 1/4 tsp. full of sea salt
- 1/4 C. full of diced almonds
- Powdered sugar for dusting

Preparation process

1. Whole milk, granulated sugar, eggs, almond essence, as well as a dash of sea salt should all be thoroughly blended in a bowl.
2. Use cooking spray or butter to grease the pot of the Ninja Speedi Cooker.
3. The cherries should be distributed equally over the pot's bottom.
4. Over the cherries, add the milk as well as egg mixture.
5. The clafoutis should be set as well as faintly browned on top after 25 Min of baking in the Speedi Cooker's Bake mode at 350°F with the lid closed.
6. Clafoutis should be taken out of the Speedi Cooker as well as given some time to cool.
7. Just before serving, top with diced almonds as well as dust with powdered sugar.

Serving Total

- Kcal:200
- Carbs: 30g
- Fat: 7g
- Protein: 5g

79. Apple as well as Cinnamon Empanadas

- Preparation Period: 20 Min
- Cooking Period: 15 Min
- Serves: 6

Ingredients needed:

For the Dough:

- 2 C. full of all-purpose flour

- 1/2 tsp. full of sea salt
- 1/2 C. full of unsea salted butter, cold as well as cubed
- 1/4 C. full of ice-cold water

For the Filling:

- 2 C. full of apples, stripped, cored, as well as diced
- 1/4 C. full of granulated sugar
- 1 tsp. full of crushed cinnamon
- 1 tbsp.full of lemon juice
- 1 tbsp.full of cornstarch

Preparation process

1. Flour as well as sea salt should be combined in a food processor. When the mixture resembles coarse crumbs, add the chilled, cubed butter as well as pulse.
2. Add the ice-cold water little by little while pulsing until the dough comes together. Refrigerate for at least 30 Min after shaping it into a disc as well as covering it in plastic wrap.
3. Apples cut into pieces, sugar, cinnamon, lemon juice, as well as cornstarch are all combined in a basin. The apples should be coated uniformly after mixing.
4. On a floured surface, roll out the cold dough to a thickness of about 1/8 inch.
5. Cut out circles from the dough using a glass or a circular cutter.
6. Each dough circle should have a small quantity of the apple filling on it.
7. To form a half-moon, fold the dough over as well as press the edges together to seal. For a decorative touch, crimp the edges using a fork.
8. The assembled empanadas should be placed inside the greased Ninja Speedi Cooker pot.
9. The empanadas should be baked for 15 Min at 375°F with the lid closed using the Speedi Cooker's Bake mode.
10. Empanadas should be taken out of the Speedi Cooker as well as given some time to cool before serving.

Serving Total

- Kcal:280
- Carbs: 35g
- Fat: 14g

- Protein: 3g

80. Lemon Blueberry pound Cake

- Preparation Period: 15 Min
- Cooking Period: 35 Min
- Serves: 6

Ingredients needed:

For the pound Cake:

- 1 1/2 C. full of all-purpose flour
- 1 1/2 tsps. full of baking powder
- 1/4 tsp. full of sea salt
- 1/2 C. full of unsea salted butter, softened
- 1 C. full of granulated sugar
- 2 huge eggs
- 1 tsp. full of vanilla extract
- 2 tbsps.full of lemon juice
- Zest of 1 lemon
- 1/2 C. full of whole milk

For the Blueberry Compote:

- 1 C. full of fresh or frozen blueberries
- 2 tbsps.full of granulated sugar
- 1 tbsp.full of lemon juice

Preparation process

1. Combine the flour, baking soda, as well as sea salt in a bowl. Place aside.
2. Cream the softened butter as well as granulated sugar in the Ninja Speedi Cooker pot until they are light as well as fluffy.
3. Add the eggs one at a time, then the lemon juice, vanilla extract, as well as lemon zest.

4. Beginning as well as ending with the dry components, add the wet elements to the dry ingredients gradually, alternating with the whole milk. Just combine after combining.
5. Blueberries, sugar, as well as lemon juice are combined in a different pan. Cook for about 5 Min, stirring periodically, over medium heat, or until the blueberries burst as well as the sauce begins to slightly thicken. Take it off the stove as well as let it cool.
6. Grease the pot of the Ninja Speedi Cooker.
7. Spread out the first half of the pound of cake batter in the pot.
8. Over the batter, spoon half of the blueberry compote.
9. Apply the remaining batter as well as blueberry compote to the same recipe.
10. A toothpick inserted into the cake should come out clean after 35 Min of baking in the Speedi Cooker's Bake mode at 350°F with the lid closed.
11. Before serving, let the lemon blueberry pound cake cool.

Serving Total

- Kcal:350
- Carbs: 50g
- Fat: 15g
- Protein: 5g

Conclusion

In the fast-paced world of modern cooking, where convenience meets quality, the Ninja Speedi Cooker has emerged as a game-changer, revolutionizing the way we prepare meals. With its advanced technology as well as versatile features, this kitchen appliance has found a place in countless homes, making cooking simpler, more efficient, as well as remarkably enjoyable.

At the heart of the Ninja Speedi Cooker's appeal is its exceptional efficiency. Designed to save both time as well as energy, it offers a wide range of cooking methods, from pressure cooking as well as baking to sautéing as well as steaming, all within a single appliance. Gone are the days of juggling multiple pots as well as pans, as the Speedi Cooker's multifunctionality allows you to create complex dishes with ease.

One of the stas well asout features of the Ninja Speedi Cooker is its intelligent cooking programs. With pre-set options for various dishes, it takes the guesswork out of cooking. Whether you're preparing a succulent roast, a creamy risotto, or a batch of fluffy rice, the Speedi Cooker's precision ensures consistently perfect results. This not only saves time but also guarantees that your culinary creations will be met with applause.

The Speedi Cooker's pressure cooking capability deserves special mention. By harnessing the power of pressure, it significantly reduces cooking times while intensifying flavors. Tough cuts of meat become tender, beans cook to perfection, as well as stews develop deep as well as rich flavors, all in a fraction of the time it would take with traditional methods. It's a culinary breakthrough that has earned the Speedi Cooker a devoted following among busy home cooks.

In our fast-paced lives, convenience is paramount. The Ninja Speedi Cooker understas well ass this as well as has been designed with convenience in mind. Its user-friendly interface, clear digital display, as well as easy-to-use controls ensure that even novice chefs can navigate the cooking process effortlessly. The non-stick pot as well as detachable parts make clean-up a breeze, as well as the sleek design adds a touch of modern elegance to any kitchen.

In an era where health-conscious cooking is a top priority, the Ninja Speedi Cooker excels. Its ability to retain nutrients while cooking under pressure ensures that your meals are not only delicious but also wholesome. You can experiment with a wide range of ingredients, from fresh vegetables to lean proteins, as well as know that you're creating meals that nourish both body as well as soul.

Beyond its practicality, the Ninja Speedi Cooker inspires culinary creativity. It encourages you to step out of your comfort zone as well as experiment with new recipes as well as flavors. The Speedi Cooker's versatility means you can try your has well as at cuisines from around the world, from hearty Indian curries to delicate French pastries, all within the confines of your own kitchen.

In conclusion, the Ninja Speedi Cooker has become more than just another kitchen appliance; it's a culinary companion that simplifies your cooking experience, enhances your culinary skills, as well as elevates your everyday meals to gourmet status. Whether you're a seasoned chef or a novice cook, the Speedi Cooker welcomes you into a world of culinary delight.

With its efficiency, precision, as well as convenience, the Ninja Speedi Cooker has undoubtedly earned its place in the modern kitchen. It has redefined the way we approach cooking, making it not just a necessity but a true pleasure. As it continues to evolve as well as inspire, it promises to be a kitchen staple for years to come, serving up delicious as well as memorable meals with every use.